GCSE OCR 21st Century
Chemistry
The Workbook

This book is for anyone doing **GCSE OCR 21st Century Chemistry** at higher level.

It's full of **tricky questions**... each one designed to make you **sweat** — because that's the only way you'll get any **better**.

There are questions to see **what facts** you know. There are questions to see how well you can **apply those facts**. And there are questions to see what you know about **how science works**.

It's also got some daft bits in to try and make the whole experience at least vaguely entertaining for you.

What CGP is all about

Our sole aim here at CGP is to produce the highest quality books — carefully written, immaculately presented and dangerously close to being funny.

Then we work our socks off to get them out to you — at the cheapest possible prices.

Contents

Module C1 — Air Quality

The Atmosphere 1
Chemical Reactions 3
Air Pollution — Carbon 4
Air Pollution — Sulfur 6
Air Pollution — Nitrogen 7
Reducing Pollution 9
Interpreting Pollution Data 10
Sustainable Development 13

Module C2 — Material Choices

Natural and Synthetic Materials 15
Materials and Properties 16
Making Measurements 17
Materials, Properties and Uses 19
Chemical Synthesis and Polymerisation 20
Structures and Properties of Polymers 22
Life Cycle Assessments 24

Module C3 — Food Matters

Recycling Elements 26
Organic and Intensive Farming 27
Pest Control 28
Natural Polymers 30
Digestion 31
Insulin and Diabetes 32
Harmful Chemicals in Food 34
Food Additives 36
Keeping Food Safe 37
Eating Healthily 39

Module C4 — Chemical Patterns

Atoms 41
Balancing Equations 42
Line Spectrums 44
The Periodic Table 45
Electron Shells 47
Group 1 — Alkali Metals 48
Group 7 — Halogens 49
Laboratory Safety 51
Ionic Bonding 52
Ions and Formulas 53

Module C5 — Chemicals of the Natural Environment

Chemicals in the Atmosphere 54
Covalent Bonding 55
Chemicals in the Hydrosphere 57
Chemicals in the Lithosphere 58
Chemicals in the Biosphere 60
Metals from Minerals 61
Electrolysis 62
Metals 64
Environmental Impact 66

Module C6 — Chemical Synthesis

Industrial Chemical Synthesis 69
Acids and Alkalis 70
Acids Reacting with Metals 72
Oxides, Hydroxides and Carbonates 73
Synthesising Compounds 75
Relative Formula Mass 78
Calculating Masses in Reactions 79
Isolating the Product and Measuring Yield 81
Titration 82
Purity 83
Rates of Reaction 84
Collision Theory 86
Measuring Rates of Reaction 87

Module C7 — Further Chemistry

Alkanes 88
Alcohols 89
Carboxylic Acids 90
Esters 91
Making an Ester 92
Energy Transfer in Reactions 93
Catalysts and Bond Energies 94
Reversible Reactions 95
Analytical Procedures 96
Analysis — Chromatography 97
Analysis — Solution Concentrations 99
Analysis — Titrations 100
The Chemical Industry 101
Producing Chemicals 102
Making Ethanol 104
Nauru and the Phosphate Industry 106

Published by Coordination Group Publications Ltd.

Editors:
Amy Boutal, Ellen Bowness, Tom Cain, Katherine Craig, Tom Harte, Sarah Hilton,
Kate Houghton, Sharon Keeley, Andy Park, Rose Parkin, Ami Snelling, Julie Wakeling.

Contributors:
Michael Aicken, Mike Bossart, Mike Dagless, Max Fishel, Richard Parsons,
Mark Pilkington, Andy Rankin, Sidney Stringer Community School,
Paul Warren, Sophie Watkins, Chris Workman.
From original material by Paddy Gannon.

ISBN: 978 1 84762 010 1

*With thanks to Jeremy Cooper, Barrie Crowther and Glenn Rogers for the proofreading.
With thanks to Laura Phillips for the copyright research.*

*Data on page 5 reproduced with kind permission from Earth System Research Laboratory,
National Oceanic and Atmospheric Administration, and Scripps Institution of Oceanography,
University of California.*

Data on page 9 reproduced courtesy of Haynes Publishing.

*Article on page 10 based on information from, "Nino Künzli, Michael Jerrett, Wendy J. Mack,
Bernardo Beckerman, Laurie LaBree, Frank Gilliland, Duncan Thomas, John Peters, and
Howard N. Hodis. Ambient Air Pollution and Atherosclerosis in Los Angeles.
Environmental Health Perspectives 113:201–206 (2005)" with kind permission from the publisher.*

Timeline on page 37 reproduced with permission from New Scientist.

*With thanks to Waste Watch, www.wastewatch.org.uk, an environmental organisation working
to change how we use the world's natural resources, for the information on page 67.*

*Data used to construct pie chart on page 69 from "Concise Dictionary of Chemistry"
edited by Daintith, J (1986). By permission of Oxford University Press. www.oup.com*

Groovy website: www.cgpbooks.co.uk

Printed by Elanders Hindson Ltd, Newcastle upon Tyne.
Jolly bits of clipart from CorelDRAW®

Text, design, layout and original illustrations © Coordination Group Publications Ltd. 2007
All rights reserved.

Module C1 — Air Quality

The Atmosphere

Q1 Complete the following passage by choosing from the words below using each word only once.

> nitrogen   oxygen   composition   carbon   1%
> constant   concentrations   water vapour   aluminium   variable

Data collected from various parts of the world has shown that the .... of nitrogen, oxygen and argon in the atmosphere are pretty much .... The current .... of the atmosphere is 78% ...., 21% .... and .... argon. There are small quantities of other gases such as .... dioxide and ....

Q2 Daniel is investigating the **air quality** in his home town.

a) Daniel took four air samples in the town centre at 12 o'clock. He analysed each one for carbon dioxide, his results are shown below. Which do you think is anomalous? Circle the correct answer.

 A 381 ppm   **B** 380 ppm   **C** 365 ppm   **D** 380 ppm

b) Suggest a reason why the anomalous result might have been obtained.

....

c) Explain why Daniel took several samples rather than just one.

....

....

Q3 a) Tick the boxes to show whether the following statements are **true** or **false**.

	True	False
i) Most of the fuels we burn in cars are carbohydrates.	☐	☐
ii) Hydrocarbons contain only carbon and hydrogen atoms.	☐	☐
iii) Diesel fuel is a compound of hydrocarbons.	☐	☐

b) Write a corrected version for the two false statements.

....

....

Module C1 — Air Quality

The Atmosphere

Q4 Different **types** of atmospheric pollution are harmful to humans in **different ways**.

a) Some pollutants are harmful in a **direct** way, meaning they cause ill health when **breathed in**. Give one possible source of this type of pollution, and a health problem it can cause.

....

....

b) Some pollutants are more harmful in an **indirect** way — for example, they may damage our environment. Describe two ways in which atmospheric pollution can damage our environment.

1. ....

....

2. ....

....

Q5 Most liquid fuels are a **mixture** of hydrocarbons. The data below shows how the **boiling points** of hydrocarbons vary with the number of carbon atoms in the molecule.

Number of carbon atoms	Boiling point /°C
5	36
6	69
7	98
8	126
10	174
11	196
12	216

a) Plot a scatter graph of this data and draw a line of best fit. *Don't forget to label the axes.*

b) Using your graph, predict the boiling point of the hydrocarbon with **nine** carbon atoms.

....

c) Describe the correlation between the number of carbon atoms and the boiling point of the hydrocarbon.

....

....

Module C1 — Air Quality

Chemical Reactions

Q1 Tick the boxes to show whether there are the correct number of atoms on either side of these equations.

correct   incorrect

a) 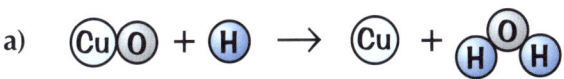 ☐ ☐

b)  ☐ ☐

c) C C + O O → C O   C O ☐ ☐

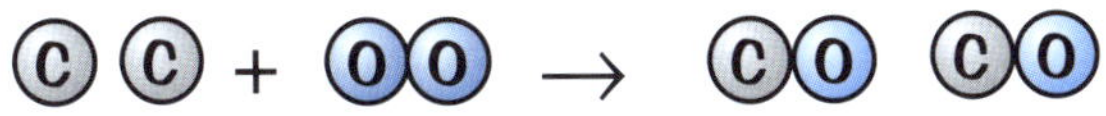

d) 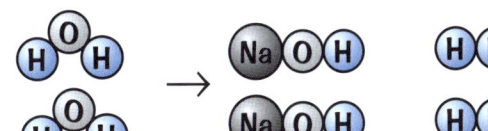 ☐ ☐

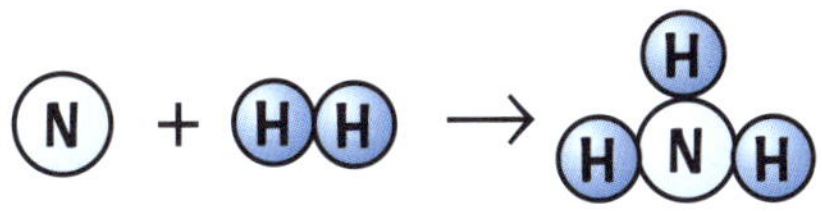

e) 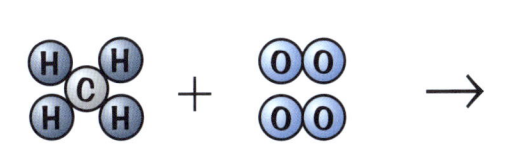 ☐ ☐

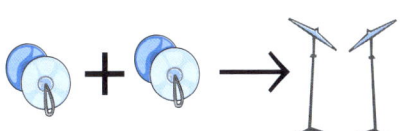

Q2 Hydrocarbons are **compounds** of **hydrogen** and **carbon** only.

a) Complete the diagram below to show what happens when the hydrocarbon methane is burnt in plenty of oxygen.

    H H C H H + O O O O O O O O →

b) What name is given to this type of reaction? ....

c) Describe what happens, in this reaction, to:

  i) the hydrogen atoms in the fuel. ....

  ....

  ii) the carbon atoms in the fuel. ....

  ....

d) How are the products of combustion different when **carbon** is burnt rather than methane?

....

Module C1 — Air Quality

Air Pollution — Carbon

Q1 Different forms of **carbon pollution** cause different problems. For each of the following give an example of a **problem** caused.

a) Carbon dioxide. ....
....

b) Carbon monoxide. ....
....

c) Particulate carbon. ....
....

Q2 The graph shows how the **carbon monoxide** concentrations in the air changed during a typical Monday in a large city.

a) On Monday mornings between 06:00 and 09:00 the **traffic** is increasingly heavy.

   i) Is there a correlation between carbon monoxide concentration and the level of traffic? Explain your answer.

   ....
   ....

   ii) Do you think that an increase in one factor causes an increase in the other? Explain your answer.

   ....
   ....

b) Would this data set convince the scientific community of a link between traffic levels and carbon monoxide concentration? Explain your answer.

   ....
   ....

c) Why is carbon monoxide produced when hydrocarbon fuel burns in a car engine?

   ....

Module C1 — Air Quality

Air Pollution — Carbon

Q3 Carbon dioxide can be removed from the atmosphere **naturally**.

a) Which process do green plants use to remove carbon dioxide from the atmosphere?

....

b) Explain why the world's **oceans** can affect atmospheric carbon dioxide levels.

....

Q4 Scientists at the Mauna Loa observatory in Hawaii have been measuring **atmospheric CO_2** levels for over **60 years**. The table shows the yearly average levels of carbon dioxide in the atmosphere from 1968 to 2000.

Year	CO_2 concentration / ppm
1968	322
1972	327
1976	332
1980	338
1984	344
1988	351
1992	355
1996	362
2000	368

a) Plot a line graph of the data.   *Don't forget to label the axes.*

b) Using your graph, estimate the concentration of carbon dioxide in 1974.

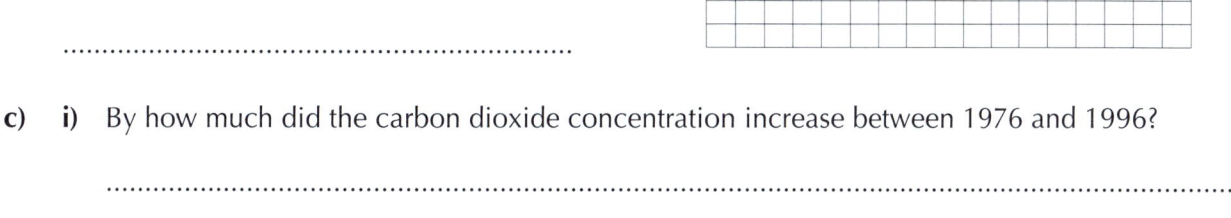

....

c) i) By how much did the carbon dioxide concentration increase between 1976 and 1996?

....

ii) Express this as a percentage increase.

....

d) All the data in the table has been shown to be **reliable**. What does this mean?

....

....

Module C1 — Air Quality

Air Pollution — Sulfur

Q1 Complete the following passage using the words below

> Coal is a **carbon** / **hydrocarbon** based fuel. Coal burnt in power stations often contains impurities — the impurity that causes the biggest problems is **silicon** / **sulfur**. When coal undergoes combustion this impurity reacts with **carbon dioxide** / **oxygen** in the air to give **sulfur dioxide** / **silicon oxide**.

Q2 Name the **compounds** described below.

a) A compound that contains two oxygen atoms joined to one sulfur atom.

....

b) A compound formed when sulfur dioxide reacts with moisture in clouds.

....

Q3 Clare is investigating how the concentration of **atmospheric pollutants** that cause acid rain affect the life span of a **limestone** headstone. She carried out the following experiment.

> 1. Pour 25 cm³ of 0.1 mol/dm³ acid into a conical flask.
> 2. Add 1 g of small limestone chips and time how long it takes for them to completely dissolve.
> 3. Repeat the experiment three times using 0.1 mol/dm³ acid.
> 4. Repeat steps 1 – 3 using more concentrated, 0.2 mol/dm³, acid instead of 0.1 mol/dm³ acid.

mol/dm³ is a unit of concentration

a) Why is it a good idea for a second scientist to carry out the experiment?

....

b) What sort of correlation should Clare expect between the concentration of acid and the time taken for the limestone chips to dissolve?

....

....

c) Give an example of an environmental problem caused by acid rain, other than damage to limestone structures.

....

....

Module C1 — Air Quality

Air Pollution — Nitrogen

Q1 Tick the boxes to show whether the following statements are **true** or **false**.

True False

a) Nitrogen pollution is formed from impurities in fuels. ☐ ☐

b) Car engines produce nitrogen pollution. ☐ ☐

c) Nitrogen dioxide combines with oxygen and water to form sulfuric acid. ☐ ☐

Q2 **Nitrogen oxides** are pollutants that can cause **acid rain**.

a) Complete the diagram to show the two stages in the formation of nitrogen dioxide from nitrogen and oxygen.

Step 1: N-N + O-O →

Step 2: + O-O →

b) Describe the conditions needed for **nitrogen monoxide** to form, and give an example of where this reaction might take place.

....

....

c) Name the product formed when nitrogen dioxide reacts with moisture in the atmosphere.

....

Q3 A scientist was investigating whether **NO$_x$** is produced during **electrical storms**. He measured the **nitric acid** concentration of the rain water produced during an electrical storm.

a) What does NO$_x$ stand for?

....

b) Explain why NO$_x$ might be produced during electrical storms?

....

c) Would it matter whether the experiment was carried out in central London or in the middle of the Yorkshire moors? Explain your answer.

....

....

d) Suggest why it will be hard to ensure the experiment is a fair test.

....

....

Module C1 — Air Quality

Air Pollution — Nitrogen

Q4 The table below shows some data about the complete combustion of three household **fuels** — coal, oil and natural gas.

Fuel	Energy output (kJ) per gram of fuel burnt	Mass of CO_2 produced (g) per gram of fuel burnt
coal	30	95
oil	48	82
natural gas	86	63

a) Which fuel produces the most energy per gram burned? ....

b) If equal amounts of all three fuels were burnt, which fuel would make the greatest contribution to the greenhouse effect? Explain your answer.

....

....

Q5 Mary measured the NO_2 concentration in the middle of a large town at 2pm on a weekday. She used ten gas analysers to sample air from the same area **simultaneously**. Her results are shown below.

Analyser	A	B	C	D	E	F	G	H	I	J
NO_2 (ppb)	21.5	21.6	21.9	22.0	21.7	21.7	21.8	24.6	21.9	21.5

a) Are any of the values anomalous? If so, which?

....

b) Suggest a possible reason for any anomalous results.

....

c) Calculate the best estimate of the true value of the NO_2 concentration.

....

d) How do you think the NO_2 concentration at 6pm the same day would be different, if at all, from the results above? Explain your answer.

....

Top Tips: The problem with atmospheric pollutants is that they generally just hang around, causing problems. And we're constantly adding more of them — which can only make things worse.

Module C1 — Air Quality

Reducing Pollution

Q1 Cars are a major source of **pollution**, though technological advances could help to **reduce** this.

a) Petrol stations now sell low-sulfur fuel. How could this help to reduce pollution?

....

b) Catalytic converters change nitrogen monoxide into which two gases?

....

c) What is the benefit of a catalytic converter changing carbon monoxide into carbon dioxide?

....

d) Suggest why it often takes a long time for pollution-reducing technologies such as catalytic converters to become widely used.

....

Q2 The best way to **reduce** CO_2 pollution is to **reduce** the amount of fossil fuels we burn.

a) One way reductions could be made is if everyone used public transport instead of cars. Suggest why this is unlikely to happen.

....

....

b) How do power stations that burn natural gas reduce sulfur dioxide pollution?

....

Q3 **Exhaust emission** checks are an important part of the **MOT test**. The test centres use a meter to check for **carbon monoxide** and **hydrocarbons**. George's car had the following test results:

	George's car	Maximum level of emissions allowed	
		Current limits (in place since 1st August 1992)	Earlier limits (in place before 1st August 1992)
Carbon monoxide level	0.2%	0.3%	3.5%
Hydrocarbon level	4 ppm	200 ppm	1200 ppm

a) Did George's car pass the emissions test?

....

b) Based on the levels of emissions allowed in the past, would you say that a modern car is more efficient than a typical car made in 1991? Explain your answer.

....

....

Module C1 — Air Quality

Interpreting Pollution Data

Q1 Read the passage below and answer the questions that follow.

Air pollution — getting to the heart of the matter

A team of scientists from the University of Southern California have found that high levels of pollution (caused by traffic and industry) could trigger atherosclerosis — the narrowing of arteries[1]. Narrowing of the arteries is caused by a thickening of the artery lining. This reduces blood flow in the artery.

Links between narrowed arteries and factors like smoking, obesity and diabetes are well established, but this report provides evidence for a link with air pollution. The study involved 798 people over the age of 40 living in the Los Angeles area. The thickness of the lining of their carotid arteries (the main artery in the neck) was measured using ultrasound.

The scientists also recorded pollution levels around the volunteers' homes. They measured the number of pollutant particles with a diameter of 2.5 micrometres or less. These particles, known as $PM_{2.5}$, are commonly produced by burning fossil fuels, e.g. petrol in cars. The levels of $PM_{2.5}$ were found to range from 5.2 to 26.9 micrograms per cubic metre ($\mu g/m^3$).

The study found that the higher the $PM_{2.5}$ level, the thicker the artery lining. On average, the artery lining was 5.9% thicker for every extra 10 $\mu g/m^3$ of $PM_{2.5}$ particles in the air. The results varied with age and sex, with the strongest link being in women over the age of 60, as shown in figure 1.

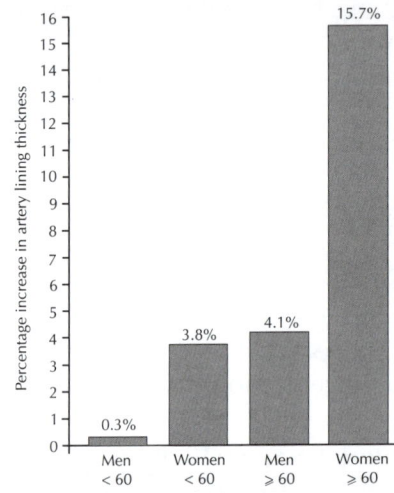

Figure 1. Percentage increase in thickness of artery lining for every 10 $\mu g/m^3$ increase in pollution.

Exactly how air pollution leads to artery narrowing is still unknown. One theory is that air pollution causes the body to produce chemicals that trigger arterial damage. Given that heart disease is now the biggest killer in many developed countries, the findings of this study could have a major influence on government decisions about public health.

[1] Nino Künzli, Michael Jerrett, Wendy J. Mack, Bernardo Beckerman, Laurie LaBree, Frank Gilliland, Duncan Thomas, John Peters, and Howard N. Hodis. Ambient Air Pollution and Atherosclerosis in Los Angeles. Environ Health Perspect 113:201-206 (2005).

Module C1 — Air Quality

Interpreting Pollution Data

a) Atherosclerosis is the build-up of fatty materials in the arteries.

   i) Circle any factors below that have been linked to atherosclerosis.

   measles   smoking   obesity   tallness   hay fever   diabetes

   ii) In which artery did the scientists measure the build-up of fatty materials?

   ....

   iii) How did the scientists measure the thickness of fatty material lining the artery?

   ....

b) The scientists measured the levels of $PM_{2.5}$ particles around the volunteers' homes.

   i) What are $PM_{2.5}$ particles?

   ....

   ....

   ii) Describe one cause of $PM_{2.5}$ pollution.

   ....

   iii) What was the lowest concentration of $PM_{2.5}$ found in the study?

   ....

   iv) According to the article, how might $PM_{2.5}$ pollution lead to arterial damage?

   ....

   ....

c) When large-scale health studies are carried out, it's usually important to include data from many different countries. Tick the box next to the most likely explanation for this.

   Scientists like to travel to different parts of the world.   ☐

   To ensure the conclusion is valid all over the world.   ☐

   To make people in other countries feel included.   ☐

Top Tips: Questions like this might seem a bit scary but the key is not to panic. You get the article before the exam so it should be familiar, and you'll be able to answer all the questions using the information in the article or what you've learnt from the rest of the specification.

Module C1 — Air Quality

Interpreting Pollution Data

d) Tick the box next to the statement which best describes what the study shows.

People living in areas of high pollution all suffer from atherosclerosis. ☐

Only people over the age of 60 will suffer from atherosclerosis. ☐

The risk of atherosclerosis is higher for people living in high pollution areas. ☐

e) The strongest link between pollution levels and artery narrowing was in women over 60. Women over 60 made up 23.3% of the volunteers.

   i) How many of the volunteers were women over 60?

   ....

   ii) A 62-year-old woman living in an area of Los Angeles with a $PM_{2.5}$ pollution level of 8.0 µg/m³ had an artery lining thickness of 100 µm. Estimate the likely artery lining thickness of a 62-year-old woman living in an area of Los Angeles with a $PM_{2.5}$ pollution level of 13 µg/m³.

   ....

   ....

   ....

   iii) A 62-year-old male had an artery lining thickness of 100 µm. He lived in an area of Los Angeles with a $PM_{2.5}$ concentration of 10 µg/m³. Another 62-year-old male had the thickness of his carotid artery lining measured as 104 µm. Estimate the $PM_{2.5}$ concentration in the area where the second man lives.

   ....

f) Some scientists feel that further large-scale studies are needed to assess the health impacts of long-term exposure to air pollution.

   i) Suggest why extra data would be helpful.

   ....

   ....

   ....

   ii) From the study described in the article, is it possible to say that 'air pollution causes atherosclerosis'? Explain your answer.

   ....

   ....

Module C1 — Air Quality

Sustainable Development

Q1 Read the following passage and answer the questions that follow.

Fuel Cells — the future of sustainability?

A fuel cell is an electrochemical device that combines hydrogen and oxygen to generate electricity. Fuel cells can be produced on any scale to give the desired power output. They have a wide range of applications — the one that interests most people is replacement of the standard car engine. Cars powered by fuel cells are basically electric cars that don't rely on batteries — they generate their own electricity.

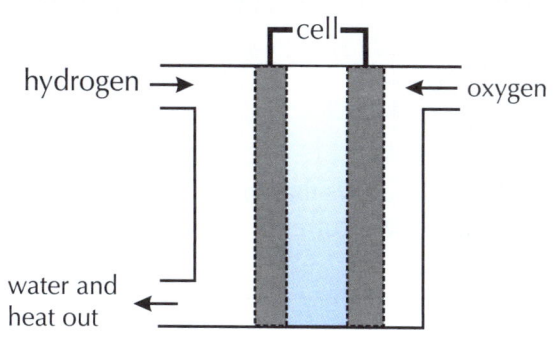

Fuel cells have the potential to reduce pollution.

With the potential to replace traditional petrol and diesel engines, fuel cells have a number of advantages:
- They produce no greenhouse gases (such as carbon dioxide), particulates or nitrogen oxide emissions. In fact the only product is water.
- Cars powered by fuel cells only use energy when they're moving, unlike a traditional car which uses fuel when stationary. Vehicles powered by a hydrogen fuel cell can be three times more efficient than those powered by petrol.
- They're very quiet compared to normal vehicle engines.

One big disadvantage is refuelling. Currently, cars powered by fuel cells can only cover a short distance before they need refuelling. However, a spokesperson for one of the large car manufacturers said that by 2010, they will have designed a fuel cell car that can go as far on a full tank as a petrol car, "without the fuel tank being twice the size of the car."

The key to making fuel cells sustainable lies with the production of the hydrogen fuel. Producing hydrogen needs a lot of energy, and this has to come from renewable energy resources such as solar, wind or biomass — or else it's still causing a lot of environmental damage.

Many see the hydrogen fuel cell as crucial in a sustainable future. It can not only reduce our dependence on oil, but will also benefit the environment by reducing emissions of greenhouse gases and pollutants that affect our air quality.

Many fuel cell powered cars are still in early stages of development so it'll be a while before we see whether they make it to mass production.

Module C1 — Air Quality

Sustainable Development

a) Fuel cells generate electrical energy from hydrogen and oxygen.

   i) Give two types of pollution that fuel cells have the potential to reduce.

   ....

   ii) What is the only product from a fuel cell?

   ....

b) The article says that the use of fuel cells would reduce our dependence on oil.
   What do we currently depend on oil for?

   ....

   ....

c) Give one way in which the standard car engine has contributed to environmental problems.

   ....

   ....

d) The fuel cell is seen by many as "crucial in a sustainable future".

   i) What is meant by the term 'sustainable development'?

   ....

   ....

   ii) Hydrogen fuel cells can produce energy for cars and a range of other applications.
   How could this help our society to develop sustainably?

   ....

   ....

   ....

   iii) Some people argue that fuel cells are not a sustainable technology because
   energy is needed to produce the hydrogen, and this energy normally comes from
   burning fossil fuels. How does the article suggest this problem can be overcome?

   ....

   ....

Module C1 — Air Quality

Module C2 — Material Choices

Natural and Synthetic Materials

Q1 Draw lines to match up each object with the probable source of the material used to make it.

- paper — silkworm larva
- leather coat — beech tree
- car tyre — cows
- silk — rubber tree

Q2 Complete the statements below using some of the following words:

| two | element | four | ions | atoms | material | mixed | bonded | mixture |

a) All materials are made up of ....

b) An .... is a chemical made up of one type of atom.

c) Water is a chemical made up of hydrogen and oxygen atoms .... together.

d) A .... contains two or more individual substances that are not chemically joined together.

Q3 Give an advantage of the following **synthetic** items compared to the **natural** alternatives.

a) Rubber seals: ....

b) Clothes: ....

c) Paints: ....

Q4 Tick the boxes to show whether the following statements are **true** or **false**.

	True	False
a) One advantage of using a synthetic material is that you can control its properties during manufacture.	☐	☐
b) It's always more expensive to use synthetic materials rather than the natural substance.	☐	☐
c) The pigment in paint is usually a natural material.	☐	☐

Top Tips: Even though all materials are made up of chemicals, some materials are natural and others are synthetic. Make sure you know the difference between these — natural materials are made from living things such as plants and animals, and synthetic materials are made by humans.

Module C2 — Material Choices

Materials and Properties

Q1 Complete the statements below by circling the correct words.

a) A weak / **strong** material is good at resisting a force.

b) You can tell how strong a material is by gradually applying a force to a sample of the material until it breaks or is temporarily / **permanently** deformed.

c) High tensile strength is when a material can resist **pulling** / pushing forces.

d) Poor compressive strength means low resistance to pulling / **pushing** forces.

e) Climbing ropes need a low / **high** tensile strength, whereas a brick low down in a wall needs a high tensile / **compressive** strength to resist the **weight** / mass of the bricks above it.

Q2 Complete the table by stating if each substance is a liquid or a solid at room temperature (20 °C).

Substance	Water	Sulfur	Propanone	Sodium chloride
Melting point (°C)	0	115	-95	801
Boiling point (°C)	100	444	56	1413
State at room temperature				

Q3 Answer the following questions about the properties of materials.

a) Explain why it is possible for a bendy material to be strong.

....

b) Steel is very stiff. Suggest why steel rods are put inside concrete posts.

....

c) Why are diamond tips used on industrial drills?

....

Q4 Use the following densities to answer the questions below.

| Gold 19.3 g/cm³ | Iron 7.9 g/cm³ | Concrete 2.6 g/cm³ |
| Cork 0.25 g/cm³ | Pine 0.5 g/cm³ | Mahogany 0.8 g/cm³ |

a) What is density?

....

b) Which materials from the list will sink when placed in water? (Water density = 1.0 g/cm³)

....

c) What will happen if a large piece of mahogany is put in a bath of water?

....

Module C2 — Material Choices

Making Measurements

Q1 Andrew and Mark conducted similar experiments to find out how **temperature** affects the **rate** of a reaction. They mixed 10 cm³ of sodium thiosulfate solution with 10 cm³ of hydrochloric acid solution to form a yellow precipitate of sulfur. The experiment involved timing how long it took for a black cross to 'disappear' through the resulting cloudy liquid.

The experiment was repeated for solutions at different temperatures. Both students followed the same method. The tables below show their results.

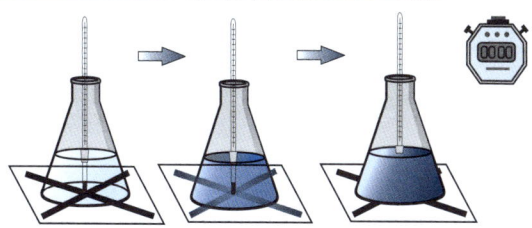

Andrew

Temperature (°C)	Time (s)			
	Trial 1	Trial 2	Trial 3	Average
20	55	59	57	
30	32	31	33	
40	21	20	19	
50	13	14	13	
60	9	8	10	

Mark

Temperature (°C)	Time (s)
20	56
30	54
40	22
50	14
60	10

a) Which pupil is likely to have the more accurate results? Explain your answer.

....

....

b) Give three ways in which they could have made sure that their experiments were fair tests.

....

....

....

c) Complete Andrew's results table by working out the average time taken at each temperature.

d) Andrew was told that the cross disappeared when 1000 mg of sulfur was formed. He can calculate **speed of the reaction** by dividing 1000 by the average time for the reaction. The units will be mg/s. For each temperature, calculate the speed of the reaction.

....

....

....

....

Module C2 — Material Choices

Making Measurements

e) i) On the grid, plot a graph of Andrew's results. Use the average time at each temperature.

   ii) Suggest why it is a good idea to use the average time when plotting a graph of Andrew's results.

   ....
   ....
   ....

   iii) Describe the correlation between temperature and time.

   ....

   iv) What conclusion can be drawn from Andrew's results?

   ....

f) Compare Andrew and Mark's results.

   i) Which of Mark's results appears to be an outlier?

   ....

   ii) Explain your choice.

   ....
   ....

   iii) Suggest how Mark could be sure that this result is an outlier.

   ....

   iv) Suggest two things that may have caused an error in Mark's results.

   ....
   ....

   v) At which temperature is there the greatest range in Andrew's results?

   ....

Module C2 — Material Choices

Materials, Properties and Uses

Q1 For each of the following questions, choose the most likely letter from the list below.

    A diving suit   B milk carton   C window pane   D washing line

  a) To which use would you put a low density opaque plastic that is hard and strong? ....

  b) To which use would you put nylon fibres that are flexible with high tensile strength? ....

  c) To which use would you put neoprene (waterproof, strong, but soft and flexible)? ....

  d) To which use would you put polycarbonate (strong, hard and transparent)? ....

Q2 Match the following sentences with their correct endings.

- Gold is suitable for jewellery because...
- uPVC is suitable for guttering pipes because...
- Stainless steel is suitable for knives and forks because...
- Lead is suitable for paperweights because...

- ...it is stiff.
- ...it is shiny.
- ...it has a high density.
- ...it is non-toxic.

Q3 The properties of different materials make them suitable for different applications.

  a) Explain why a tennis racket is made with a **metal frame** and **nylon strings**.

      ....

      ....

  b) Explain why a saucepan is made with **a metal body** and **wooden handle**.

      ....

      ....

Q4 A mystery material has just been discovered. It has a **high melting point**, **high tensile strength** and **low density**, and is also **flexible**, **soft**, **non-toxic** and **flame resistant**.

  a) Put a ring around the product that this material would be most suitable for.

      knives and forks   guttering   children's nightwear   synthetic candle wax

  b) Explain how one of the properties of the 'mystery' substance make it suitable for your choice.

      ....

  c) For one of the other products give two reasons why the mystery material would **not** be suitable.

      1. ....

      2. ....

Module C2 — Material Choices

Chemical Synthesis and Polymerisation

Q1 Tick the boxes to show whether the statements are **true** or **false**.

		True	False
a)	Fossil fuels are formed from dead plants and animals.	☐	☐
b)	Hydrocarbons contain carbon and water only.	☐	☐
c)	A lot of the crude oil we extract is used for providing energy.	☐	☐
d)	Polymerisation is the process of converting long hydrocarbons into shorter ones.	☐	☐

Q2 Complete the following passage by choosing from the words below.

varying   synthetic   mixture   chains   modified   natural
compounds   equal   diesel   plastics   refines   small

Crude oil is a .... of lots of different hydrocarbons. These molecules are .... of atoms of .... lengths. The petrochemical industry .... crude oil to produce petrol, ... and other fuels and lubricants. A very .... amount of the crude oil is used to make .... substances — man-made .... such as ...., medicines and fertilisers.

Q3 Bob runs an **oil refinery plant**. He is comparing the percentages of each fraction produced in his plant with his customers' demand. His results are shown in the table.

Fraction	Refinery gas	Petrol and naphtha	Kerosene	Diesel	Oil and Bitumen
% of production	3	15	12	21	49
% of demand	5	28	9	24	34

Fractions are the different types of chemical that crude oil is split into.

a) Which fractions are currently in greater demand than is available?

....

b) What is likely to be the greatest use of these fractions?

....

Top Tips: Crude oil is a mixture of hydrocarbons, and it's a pretty useless substance on its own. However, refined crude oil is useful for loads of different things because each fraction has different properties. They can be cracked to produce even more of the useful substances.

Module C2 — Material Choices

Chemical Synthesis and Polymerisation

Q4 For each of the following questions give the most likely answer from A–D.

a) Polymerisation is best described as ....

    A lots of small molecules joining to form long chains

    B lots of large molecules joining to form long chains

    C a small number of molecules joining together

    D two molecules joining together to form one molecule

b) Polymers are among the most important .... materials.

    A synthetic   B biodegradable   C natural   D black

c) Polymers are usually .... based.

    A sodium   B sulfur   C carbon   D argon

d) Polymers are formed when small molecules are mixed under conditions of .... pressure.

    A low   B medium   C high   D zero

Q5 The uses of polymers depend on their properties.

a) Suggest three properties that a polymer used to make window frames should have.

....

b) Suggest two properties of high density polythene which make it suitable for washing-up bowls.

....

c) Suggest why polystyrene foam is used for disposable tea cups.

....

d) Suggest three properties of polypropene which make it suitable for use in plastic kettles.

....

Q6 Over time, materials used to make common items can be replaced with different materials.

a) Suggest one advantage of using PVC rather than wood for window frames.

....

b) Suggest two advantages of replacing paper bags with plastic bags.

....

....

Module C2 — Material Choices

Structures and Properties of Polymers

Q1 Complete the following passage by circling the correct words.

> Polymer chains are held **together** / **apart** by forces between the chains. If these forces are weak, the chains **cannot** / **can** slide over each other easily. This makes the polymer **inflexible** / **flexible** and gives it a **low** / **high** melting point. The stronger the bonds between the polymer chains, the **more** / **less** energy is needed to break them apart, and the **lower** / **higher** the melting point.

Q2 Polymers can be **modified** to give them different properties.

a) In what four ways can polymers be modified to change their properties?

1. .... 2. ....

3. .... 4. ....

b) Describe how a polymer's properties would change if its chain length was increased.

....

....

c) Explain how adding cross-linking agents affects the properties of a polymer.

....

....

Q3 uPVC is strong, durable and rigid. When another chemical is added to the uPVC, it becomes stretchy, soft and easier to shape. It can then be used as **synthetic leather**.

a) What is the general name given to chemicals that can be added to polymers to make them softer and more pliable?

....

b) Explain how these chemicals make the polymer softer.

....

....

Module C2 — Material Choices

Structures and Properties of Polymers

Q4 Read the following passage and then answer the questions.

In America in the early 1830s natural rubber was used to make various things. However, in hot weather it turned into a glue-like mess as it 'melted'. Charles Goodyear experimented by adding different substances to the rubber to try to improve its properties. By accident, he found that heating rubber with sulfur produced a hardened version of the rubber. He called the process vulcanization and set up a business making tyres.

a) What is the process of hardening rubber by adding sulfur called?

....

b) What is the cross-linking agent in this process?

....

c) Describe how adding a cross-linking agent changed the properties of the rubber.

....

....

Q5 Polymers can have a **crystalline** or a **non-crystalline** structure.

a) State whether the diagrams show a crystalline or a non-crystalline plastic.

i) ii)

....

b) Describe the structure of a non-crystalline polymer.

....

....

c) Describe the structure of a crystalline polymer.

....

....

d) Give three properties of crystalline polymers.

....

Top Tips: A polymer's properties depend on how its chains are arranged and how they're held together. But — don't forget that polymers can be modified to change their properties. You'd better get modifying the contents of your brain to include this stuff, 'cos this could come up in the exam...

Module C2 — Material Choices

Life Cycle Assessments

Q1 Complete the passage using the words below. *Each word can only be used once.*

> stage   cycle   environment   assess   laws   governments
> sustainable   process   materials   protect   cost

The business of manufacturing things is changing as new .... are being introduced. Companies have to .... the impact their processes and products will have on the .... and use this information to choose a .... that does minimal harm. It also helps them to choose the best .... for the job. They have to look at the impact of each .... of the product's life — this is known as a Life .... Assessment. Data from the Life Cycle Assessment enables companies to help .... future generations.

Q2 Which stages of a product's life are being described below? Match them up.

A computer being powered by electricity.	Using the product.
Polythene being made from ethene.	Disposing of the product.
A lot of plastic bottles being thrown away.	Extracting the raw materials.
Oil being drilled out of the ground.	Manufacturing the product.

Q3 Tick the boxes to show whether the statements are **true** or **false**.   True False

a) A Life Cycle Assessment can't help in deciding the best raw materials to use. ☐ ☐

b) Generally, the extraction of raw materials needs energy. ☐ ☐

c) Companies always include cost as one of the factors to think about. ☐ ☐

d) The quantity of available raw materials should be ignored in an Life Cycle Assessment. ☐ ☐

e) Recycling materials at the disposal stage is more sustainable than putting them in landfill. ☐ ☐

Module C2 — Material Choices

Life Cycle Assessments

Q4 Governments in poorer countries are often less strict about environmental concerns when manufacturing products.

Suggest a reason for this.

....

....

Q5 The length of a product's life cycle can vary quite a bit.

Compare a plastic drinks bottle with a plastic garden chair.

a) Which product is likely to have the longest life-span?

....

b) Which product is likely to cost more to manufacture?

....

c) Which product is more likely to be recycled rather than being put into landfill?

....

Q6 A Life Cycle Assessment can tell a company if it's possible to make a product and what the environmental impact will be. However, it can't tell the company whether it **should** make the product.

Suggest two other things that companies may consider when deciding whether to manufacture a product.

....

....

....

Q7 Suggest three benefits a company might get from doing a Life Cycle Assessment.

1. ....

2. ....

3. ....

Top Tips: Life Cycle Assessments do just what you'd expect them to do — they look at each stage of the life cycle of a potential product to assess the impact that it would have on the environment. Get that sorted and it'll be one less assessment to think about...

Module C2 — Material Choices

Recycling Elements

Q1 Use these words to complete the blanks.

feeding   soil   microbes   cycling   decompose   leaves   roots

There is a continual .... of elements on Earth. In plants, elements are taken in through the .... and .... Animals take in elements through .... and respiration. Elements are returned to the environment when animals excrete (poo) or when animals and plants die and .... This process of decay is carried out by .... , such as bacteria. The elements released by decay either enter the .... or go into the air, where they can be taken up again by other living organisms.

Q2 Plants take in **elements** and **compounds** from the environment.

a) Give three elements that are constantly recycled through living organisms.

....

b) Describe how an element present in the **soil** can become part of an animal.

....

....

c) Name one type of molecule that plants use **nitrates** to make.

....

Q3 Circle the correct word(s) to complete the sentences below.

a) Nitrogen gas in the atmosphere is turned into nitrates by **nitrifying / nitrogen-fixing** bacteria.

b) Bacteria that convert organic waste, such as rotting plants, into ammonium compounds are called **nitrogen-fixing bacteria / decomposers**.

c) Ammonium compounds are turned into useful nitrates by **nitrifying / nitrogen-fixing** bacteria.

d) Nitrates in the soil are turned back into nitrogen gas in the air by **denitrifying bacteria / decomposers**.

Q4 Bacteria can turn nitrogen in the air into **nitrates** in the soil.

Name another way that nitrogen in the air can be turned into nitrates in the soil.

....

Organic and Intensive Farming

Q1 Elements are lost from the soil when crops are harvested.

a) Name three important chemical elements that are lost from the soil.

....

b) What happens to the fertility of the soil if these elements are not replaced? ....

c) Use the words given below to complete the passage.

fertile   cycle   sewage   manure   crop rotation

> Organic farmers keep their fields .... by replacing lost elements
> in the soil. For example, they spread ...., compost or human
> .... on the land. They also use ...., which
> means that they grow a different crop each year in a ....

d) Organic farmers may grow 'green manure'. Explain what this means.

....

e) How do intensive farmers replace elements lost from the soil?

....

Q2 A farmer grows a crop of maize in a field for six consecutive years. The **yield** of maize each year is recorded in the bar chart.

a) Describe the trend shown by the data, and suggest a reason for it.

....

....

b) One year's yield doesn't fit the trend. Which year is it? Suggest a reason for this result.

....

Q3 Intensive farming relies on **artificial fertilisers**.

a) Give three advantages of using artificial fertilisers rather than organic methods.

....

....

b) Explain why an organic farmer may choose to grow peas in a field the year before he grows cabbages there.

....

Module C3 — Food Matters

Pest Control

Q1 Tick the boxes to show whether the statements are **true** or **false**.

True False
a) Pests and disease can greatly reduce crop yields. ☐ ☐
b) Ladybirds are pests that can affect crops. ☐ ☐
c) Potato blight is a disease that can kill crop plants. ☐ ☐
d) Crop rotation can be used to control pests and disease. ☐ ☐

Q2 Choose from the words below to complete the passage.

control   resist   biological processes   wide   crop rotation   pesticides   predators   narrow

Organic farmers can use .... to deal with pests and disease. For example, they can use natural .... to biologically .... pests such as greenfly. .... helps to prevent the pests and diseases of one particular crop building up in an area. Varieties of plants can be grown that are best able to .... pests and diseases. .... field edges can be left uncultivated to encourage larger insects and other animals that feed on pests.

Q3 Intensive farmers use **man-made** chemical pesticides.

a) Give two advantages of using man-made chemical pesticides to treat crops.

....

....

b) How could pesticide spraying cause harm to humans who consume the crop?

....

c) What effect might chemical pesticides have on ecosystems in or near to the crops being sprayed?

....

Module C3 — Food Matters

Pest Control

Q4 Sameer and Philippa compare the prices of chicken in a supermarket. An **organic** chicken costs £8.99, a **non-organic free-range** chicken costs £6.99, while a **non-organic** chicken raised by **intensive battery farming** costs £3.99. All three are the same size.

Suggest three reasons why there is a difference in price.

Think about animal welfare, growth promotion, and feeding costs.

....

....

....

....

....

Q5 A company tested a new fertiliser, **Fert X**, to see whether it produced a better crop yield than their existing fertiliser, **OldFert**. A field was divided into two equal areas and cabbages were planted in both. In area A, 50 kg of Fert X was applied, and in area B 50 kg of OldFert was applied. After three months, the cabbages were harvested and the mass of cabbages produced from each area recorded. Area A produced a **higher yield** of cabbages than area B.

a) Give three controlled variables in this experiment.

....

....

b) Suggest two reasons why this experiment might not have been a fair test.

....

....

c) The company decides not to produce and sell Fert X. Suggest two reasons, one economic and one environmental, why they may have made this decision.

....

....

d) The company draws the conclusion that 'Both Fert X and OldFert are effective fertilisers for cabbages.' Are they right to say this based on the trial above? If not, what further experiment would they need to do?

....

....

Module C3 — Food Matters

Natural Polymers

Q1 Polymers are formed from the combination of lots of smaller molecules known as **monomers**.

Name two groups of compounds that are natural polymers.

....

Q2 Carbohydrates can be monomers or polymers.

a) Circle the elements below that are found in **carbohydrates**.

nitrogen   carbon   oxygen   sulfur   sodium   hydrogen   gold

b) Are the following monomers or polymers? Tick the correct box in each case.

	Monomer	Polymer
i) cellulose	☐	☐
ii) glucose	☐	☐
iii) starch	☐	☐

c) What is the name of the process plants use to produce glucose from carbon dioxide and water?

....

Q3 Label the monomers in these diagrams.

a) .... → protein

b) .... → starch

Q4 Tick the boxes to show whether the statements are **true** or **false**.

		True	False
a)	Amino acids join together to form proteins.	☐	☐
b)	Proteins contain the elements carbon, hydrogen, oxygen and nitrogen.	☐	☐
c)	There are about 200 different amino acids used in the human body.	☐	☐
d)	Plants take in proteins from the soil.	☐	☐
e)	Amino acids are polymers.	☐	☐

Module C3 — Food Matters

Digestion

Q1 Circle the correct words to complete the sentences below.

a) Food is made up of small / big molecules such as starch, proteins, and fats.

b) Digestion is the process of breaking down / building up large molecules.

c) Small molecules that are soluble / insoluble can enter the blood.

d) Big insoluble molecules are digested in the small / large intestine.

Q2 Match up the foods with the polymers they contain, and the monomers they're made up of.

bread / potatoes / muesli   starch   amino acids

meat / eggs / fish   proteins   glucose molecules

Q3 There are an enormous number of different **proteins** in the human body, yet there are only a small number of different **amino acids**.

a) Explain how amino acids are able to form this huge variety of proteins.

....

b) Give four parts of the body that are mainly made of proteins.

....

Q4 Use the words below to fill in the blanks in the passage.

| urine | liver | blood | excreted | urea |
| proteins | excess | kidneys | growing |

Amino acids are transported around the body in the .... They are

taken up by .... cells which need them to make ....

Any amino acids that cannot be used at once have to be .... These

.... amino acids are taken to the .... where they are

converted into .... This is taken by the blood to the ....,

where it is passed out in the ....

Module C3 — Food Matters

Insulin and Diabetes

Q1 Diabetes is a disorder involving the hormone **insulin**.

a) Which organ in the human body produces insulin? ....

b) How does insulin help to control blood sugar levels?

....

c) Circle the correct words to complete the paragraph below.

> When you eat foods that contain a lot of sugar, the sugar enters your bloodstream **slowly** / **quickly**, making your blood sugar level **rise** / **fall** very quickly. Instead of sugary foods, dietitians recommend that you should eat foods that contain complex **carbohydrates** / **proteins** like **rice** / **chocolate**, which are gradually broken down into **fat** / **sugar** by the body.

Q2 Nigel is a trainee doctor. As part of his training he is presented with case studies of two patients.

> Patient X is 50 years old. She has visited the doctor to complain of increasing tiredness, constant thirst and a frequent need to 'visit the toilet for a wee'. On questioning, she admits to a poor diet, based on processed foods and sugar-rich soft drinks, and she is overweight. A urine test and a blood test show that she has abnormally high blood glucose levels.

> Patient Y is 6 years old. She has been taken to hospital suffering from nausea and vomiting. Her symptoms have developed suddenly. She is severely dehydrated and close to falling into a coma. A blood test shows that she has abnormally high glucose levels. Patient Y's parents state that prior to this emergency, she had seemed a healthy child.

a) i) Which patient may have type 1 diabetes? ....

ii) Explain your answer. ....

....

b) What advice on lifestyle should the doctor give Patient X?

....

Top Tips: Normally, insulin (which lowers blood sugar levels) is produced in response to an increase in blood sugar level. Diabetics can't control their blood sugar levels properly using insulin, so it's really important for them to control their diet — to try and keep their sugar levels stable.

Module C3 — Food Matters

Insulin and Diabetes

Q3 Choose from the words below to complete the passages about diabetes.

pancreas   diet   death   weekly   weight   sugar   enough
insulin   younger   responding   daily   high   brain   older

a) Type 1 diabetes usually develops in .... people, when the .... stops producing .... Blood .... levels can become so .... that they damage the body, possibly causing coma and .... This type of diabetes can be controlled with .... injections of insulin.

b) Type 2 diabetes usually affects .... people. It develops either because the body stops making .... insulin or because the body stops .... to it normally. Type 2 diabetes is controlled by improving the ...., losing .... and exercising.

Q4 Why is type 2 diabetes becoming more common in young people?

....

....

Q5 Thelma finishes eating a meal at 12 o'clock, and her blood sugar (glucose) levels are monitored for the next three hours. The results are shown on the graph.

a) What is the normal blood glucose level in Thelma's blood?

....

b) By how much does her blood glucose rise after the meal?

....

c) How long does it take after finishing the meal for Thelma's blood glucose level to return to normal?

....

d) Thelma's pancreas works normally at the moment. If Thelma developed diabetes and her body stopped producing enough insulin, predict two differences that you might notice on the graph for a similar experiment.

....

....

Module C3 — Food Matters

Harmful Chemicals in Food

Q1 Draw lines to match the foods with the dangers associated with them.

uncooked cassava

proteins in peanuts

gluten in wheat

rashes, swellings, vomiting, diarrhoea and breathing problems

cyanide poisoning

rash and swelling of the mouth and throat

Q2 In farming, both **pesticides** and **herbicides** are widely used. Pesticides are used to kill insects and other pest organisms.

a) Why might residues of pesticides and herbicides be found in the food we eat?

....

b) Many parents now feed their babies with organic baby food. Suggest why they might have taken this precaution.

....

....

Q3 Some foods can become contaminated with **aflatoxin** if they're not stored properly.

a) Give two examples of foods that are prone to contamination with aflatoxin if stored incorrectly.

....

b) What produces the aflatoxin in these foods?

....

c) Give one health problem that can be caused by eating food containing aflatoxin.

....

d) Explain why it may be dangerous for humans to eat food produced for animals, such as bird seed.

....

Top Tips: It's important to remember that just because something is eaten very commonly, it's not necessarily completely safe. Some foods are naturally dangerous. Some contain potentially harmful chemicals from farming. Others develop dangerous chemicals during storage or cooking.

Module C3 — Food Matters

Harmful Chemicals in Food

Q4 Harmful chemicals can be formed when **cooking** foods.

a) Name two harmful chemicals that can be produced when food is cooked at high temperatures.
....

b) How do these chemicals cause cancer when consumed by animals?
....

c) Give three ways of reducing the amounts of these harmful chemicals in your diet.
....
....

d) It is known that grilling meat at high temperatures produces harmful chemicals. Why do many people still cook meat this way? Give three reasons.
....
....
....

Q5 Potatoes produce a toxic chemical called **solanine**, which is present in high levels in the potato plant's leaves and shoots. The potato itself has a relatively low level of solanine, but this level can rise if it is not stored properly. **Green** potatoes are an indicator of high levels of solanine. Solanine concentrates especially in the **potato skin**, and cannot be removed by washing or cooking.

For an average person, a lethal dose of solanine can be about 5 milligrams per kilogram of body mass. Even correctly stored potatoes can contain about 200 milligrams per kilogram.

a) Calculate the dose of solanine that would be lethal for a 50 kg person.
....

b) What mass of potatoes would need to be eaten to produce this lethal dose?
....

c) Suggest how to prepare potatoes in order to reduce the amounts of solanine eaten.
....

d) Give two reasons why potatoes aren't banned by the Government or the European Union, even though they contain such high levels of dangerous chemicals.
....
....

Module C3 — Food Matters

Food Additives

Q1 Lots of foods contain additives.

a) Why are **food colours** added to some foods? ....

b) What is the difference between **flavourings** and **flavour enhancers**?

....

....

c) Why are diet drinks made with artificial sweeteners?

....

Q2 Choose from these words to complete the blanks. foul-smelling   sodium benzoate   antioxidants
oxygen   rancid   preservatives   nitrogen

Foods that contain fats or oils can go off by reacting with ....

in the air. Butter can go .... as the oxygen breaks down the

fat into .... products. To prevent this from happening,

chemicals called .... are added to food containing fats or oils.

Other foods can have ...., such as ....,

added to prevent the growth of harmful microbes.

Q3 **Emulsifiers** and **stabilisers** can be added to certain foods.

a) Why are emulsifiers necessary in some foods?

....

b) What are stabilisers used in foods for?

....

Q4 Some food additives are thought to cause health problems.

a) If a food additive has been given an **E number**, what does this mean?

....

b) Why might a food additive with an E number **not** be allowed to be used in the USA or Canada?

....

c) Give three health problems linked to food additives.

....

....

Module C3 — Food Matters

Keeping Food Safe

Q1 Read the information below and then answer the questions that follow.

> Bovine spongiform encephalopathy (BSE) is a cattle disease that first appeared in Britain in the mid-1980s. It leads to a fatal degeneration of brain function. The early symptoms of disorientation and shakiness caused it to be popularly termed 'mad cow disease'.
>
> A probable link between BSE and a newly discovered fatal brain disease in humans, variant Creutzfeldt-Jakob Disease (vCJD), was found, leading to an international crisis about the safety of British beef for human consumption.

This timeline shows how the problem developed:

- **December 1984** — A cow on a farm in Sussex becomes the first confirmed victim of BSE, dying early in 1985. Other cows begin to show the same symptoms.
- **November 1986** — BSE becomes recognised as a new cattle disease.
- **October 1987** — BSE is found to be similar to the existing disease, scrapie, in sheep. Scientists begin suggesting that BSE may be caused by feeding cattle with protein derived from the carcasses of other animals, such as sheep.
- **July 1988** — Many animal proteins are banned from sheep and cattle feed.
- **February 1989** — An expert scientific committee, the Spongiform Encephalopathy Advisory Committee (SEAC), is established.
- **November 1989** — Certain forms of bovine offal, such as brains and spleens, are banned from human foods.
- **May 1990** — A pet cat is found to have a BSE-like disease. This is the first indication (outside a lab) that BSE might be able to infect a different species.
- **1992/1993** — BSE reaches a peak, affecting 0.3% of Britain's cattle.
- **May 1995** — The first person dies from vCJD.
- **March 1996** — SEAC announces a probable link between BSE in cattle and vCJD in humans. News reports give predictions of human deaths in the UK from vCJD that range from hundreds to tens of thousands.
- **March 1996** — The EU (European Union) bans British beef exports.
- **August 1996** — Cattle most at risk from BSE are slaughtered.
- **February 2003** — Predicted deaths from vCJD are now thought to be at worst 7000.
- **December 2004** — Total number of people in Britain with vCJD reaches 150.

Module C3 — Food Matters

Keeping Food Safe

a) Tick the boxes to show whether the following sentences are **data** or **explanations**.

    Data Explanation

  i) The pet cat had a disease similar to BSE. ☐ ☐

  ii) BSE was able to jump the species barrier and infect a pet cat. ☐ ☐

b) Give two measures that were taken to prevent the spread of BSE.

....

....

c) i) Using ideas about **feasibility**, **risk** and **benefit**, suggest why the British Government never decided to completely ban beef for human consumption.

....

....

....

  ii) What is likely to have caused the EU to ban British beef exports in 1996?

....

d) In 1992/1993 there were about 12 000 000 cattle in the UK. Approximately how many were affected by BSE?

....

e) The first person died from vCJD relatively late into the BSE crisis. Suggest why scientists couldn't accurately predict, in 1996, how many people would die from vCJD.

....

....

f) In December 2003, a British man died from vCJD, which he was thought to have developed following a blood transfusion seven years earlier. Many countries took action to ban people who had lived in Britain during the BSE crisis from being **blood donors**.

  i) Use the idea of the '**precautionary principle**' to explain why some countries took that action.

....

....

  ii) Suggest why the UK Blood Service did not implement a similar ban.

....

....

Module C3 — Food Matters

Eating Healthily

Q1 Read the following newspaper article and then answer the questions that follow.

'Fish Oil Supplements Boost Exam Performance' August 2005

It has been long established in folk wisdom that a healthy body leads to a healthy mind. One school in Sheepshire has put this claim to the test by giving all its Year 11 students daily fish oil supplements in the year running up to their GCSEs.

Thomasina Gradgrind, head teacher of Thwackum School, said that the improvements have been remarkable. "In 2004, 40% of our candidates achieved at least five A*-C grades at GCSE. But this year, following the use of the fish oil supplements, we have seen this boosted to 50%."

There has been huge media interest in the school's project and many of the students have featured in local and national newspapers. One student, Kyle, was the subject of a documentary on national TV. "It was amazing," he said. "I used to hate school and often played truant. But this year, I settled down and studied hard for my exams. I'm really pleased with my results, and I'm hoping to begin a training course at college in September."

The fish oil capsules given to the students are rich in omega-3 fatty acids, which scientists believe to be essential for brain function. These fatty acids are found in oily fish such as sardines and mackerel but are often lacking in the diet of many people.

However, a leading scientist in the study of how diet affects behaviour, Professor Carlos Carlosson of Ox-fridge University, expressed doubts about the results. "I was disappointed to see that there was no proper control, and that the use of 'dummy' pills had not been included in the study. Besides, the media attention may have biased the results."

Ms Gradgrind dismisses the criticism and remains convinced of the positive effects of fish oil pills. "I would like to thank all my students and staff. Everyone has made a special effort this year, and the results are terrific!"

---

a) Use the information in the article, and your knowledge of scientific ideas, to consider whether the following statements are **true**, **false**, or you **can't say**.

     True False Can't say

i) The GCSE results improved at Thwackum School from 2004 to 2005.

ii) Fish oil supplements improve exam performance.

iii) Some students at Thwackum School took 'dummy' pills during the study.

iv) Key Stage 3 students given fish oil supplements will get better results, on average, in their SATs.

v) Further studies are needed to give greater confidence in the connection between fish oil supplements and exam performance.

b) One of Professor Carlosson's concerns is that Thwackum School doesn't have many students in each year group compared to many other schools.
Why might he be concerned about the number of students involved in this study?

....

Module C3 — Food Matters

Eating Healthily

c) A new homework club and Saturday tuition for GCSE Maths, English and Science were introduced at the same time as the fish oil pills. Why is this a flaw in the design of the experiment?

    ....

    ....

d) Professor Carlosson is concerned that **media attention** may have biased the study.
    How might this attention have influenced the behaviour of the students, parents and teachers?

    Students: ....

    Parents: ....

    Teachers: ....

e) Professor Carlosson thinks that while fish oil pills are an excellent source of omega-3 fatty acids, it is better for people to get their omega-3 fatty acids from a healthy balanced diet.
    Suggest why this might be the case.

    ....

    ....

f) Professor Carlosson conducts a new study into the influence of fish oil supplements on GCSE exam performance. He selects at random 50% of the students to take **fish oil supplements** during Year 11. The other 50% of students are given **'dummy'** pills. No student is told which type of pill they are being given. Their GCSE Maths results are shown in the graph.

    i) How many students in total were involved in this study?

        ....

        ....

    ii) Calculate the percentage of students obtaining grades A*-C in each group.

        Students taking fish oil pills: ....

        ....

        Students taking 'dummy' pills: ....

        ....

    iii) Despite the higher number of students taking the fish oil supplements obtaining grades A*-C, Professor Carlosson doesn't think these results provide evidence that fish oils improve Maths performance. Other than fish oils, suggest an explanation for this higher number.

        ....

        ....

Module C3 — Food Matters

Module C4 — Chemical Patterns

Atoms

Q1 Draw a diagram of a **helium atom** in the space provided and label each type of **particle** on your diagram.

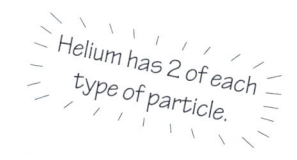

Helium has 2 of each type of particle.

Q2 **Complete** this table.

Particle	Mass	Charge
Proton	1	
		0
Electron	0.0005	

Q3 **Complete** the following sentences.

a) Neutral atoms have a charge of ....

b) A charged atom is called an ....

c) A neutral atom has the same number of .... and ....

d) If an electron is added to a neutral atom, the atom becomes .... charged.

e) The number of .... in an atom tells you what element it is.

f) In a neutral atom, the number of protons is equal to the number of ....

Q4 Complete the table below to show the number of **protons** and **electrons** in atoms.

element	electrons	protons
magnesium	12	
carbon		6
oxygen		

Use a periodic table to help you with this question.

Module C4 — Chemical Patterns

Balancing Equations

Q1 Which of the following equations are **balanced** correctly? Tick the correct boxes.

		Correctly balanced	Incorrectly balanced
a)	$H_2 + Cl_2 \rightarrow 2HCl$	☐	☐
b)	$CuO + HCl \rightarrow CuCl_2 + H_2O$	☐	☐
c)	$N_2 + H_2 \rightarrow NH_3$	☐	☐
d)	$CuO + H_2 \rightarrow Cu + H_2O$	☐	☐
e)	$CaCO_3 \rightarrow CaO + CO_2$	☐	☐

Q2 Here is the equation for the formation of **carbon monoxide** in a poorly ventilated gas fire. It is **not** balanced correctly.

$$C + O_2 \rightarrow CO$$

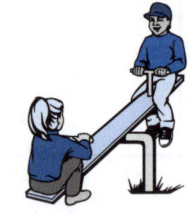

Alice and Bob were incorrectly balanced.

Circle the **correctly balanced** version of this equation.

$$C + O_2 \rightarrow CO_2$$
$$C + O_2 \rightarrow 2CO$$
$$2C + O_2 \rightarrow 2CO$$

Q3 **Sodium** (Na) reacts with **water** (H_2O) to produce **sodium hydroxide** (NaOH) and **hydrogen** (H_2).

a) What are the **reactants** and the **products** in this reaction?

Reactants: .... Products: ....

b) Write the **word equation** for this reaction.

....

c) Write the **balanced symbol equation** for the reaction.

....

d) What state symbol would be used in the equations above for:

  i) water? ....   ii) hydrogen gas? ....

Top Tips: The most important thing to remember with balancing equations is that you **can't** change the **little numbers** — if you do that then you'll change the substance into something completely different. Right, now that I've given you that little gem of knowledge, you can carry on with the rest. Just take your time and work through everything logically.

Module C4 — Chemical Patterns

Balancing Equations

Q4 Write out the balanced **symbol** equations for the picture equations below (some of which are unbalanced).

a) Na + Cl₂ → NaCl

$2Na + Cl_2 \rightarrow 2NaCl$

b) Li + O₂ → Li₂O

$4Li + O_2 \rightarrow 2Li_2O$

c) MgCO₃ + HCl → MgCl₂ + H₂O + CO₂

$MgCO_3 + 2HCl \rightarrow MgCl_2 + H_2O + CO_2$

d) Li + H₂O → LiOH + H₂

$2Li + 2H_2O \rightarrow 2LiOH + H_2$

Q5 Add **one** number to each of these equations so that they are **correctly balanced**.

a) ...... CuO + ... HBr → ...... CuBr₂ + ... H₂O

b) ...... H₂ + ... Br₂ → ...... HBr

c) ...... Mg + ... O₂ → 2MgO

d) 2NaOH + ... H₂SO₄ → ...... Na₂SO₄ + ... H₂O

Q6 **Balance** these equations by adding in numbers.

a) ...... NaOH + ... AlBr₃ → ...... NaBr + ... Al(OH)₃

b) ...... FeCl₂ + ... Cl₂ → ...... FeCl₃

c) ...... N₂ + ... H₂ → ...... NH₃

d) ...... Fe + ... O₂ → ...... Fe₂O₃

e) ...... NH₃ + ... O₂ → ...... NO + ... H₂O

$Fe_2O_3 + 3CO \rightarrow 2Fe + 3CO_2$

Module C4 — Chemical Patterns

Line Spectrums

Q1 A scientist is carrying out a **flame test** to identify the **metals** in three different compounds.

a) Complete the following sentence about flame testing.

> Some elements give a distinctive ....
> when placed in a ....

b) Draw lines to match the flame colours the scientist sees to the metal that is present.

- lithium
- sodium
- potassium

- yellow/orange
- red
- lilac

Q2 a) Use the words in the box to complete the passage about **line spectrums**. Some words may be used more than once.

| light | element | line |
| elements | excited | electron | electrons |

When heated, the .... in an atom become .... and release energy as .... The wavelengths of .... emitted can be recorded as a .... spectrum. Different .... emit different wavelengths of .... due to their different .... arrangements. This means that each .... will produce a different .... spectrum, allowing them to be identified.

b) As well as to help identify compounds, what else have line spectrums been used for?

....

Top Tips: I don't know why atoms get so excited at the prospect of being stuck in a hot flame — it certainly doesn't appeal to me. There's no accounting for some tastes... Anyway, line spectrums aren't as tricky as they might seem at first. Stick at it — they could easily come up in the exam — and you'll be passing with, errr... flying colours...

Module C4 — Chemical Patterns

The Periodic Table

Q1 Use a **periodic table** to help you answer the following questions.

a) Name one element in the same period as silicon. ....

b) Name one element in the same group as potassium. ....

c) Name one element that is a halogen. ....

d) Name one element that is an alkali metal. ....

Q2 **Complete** this table.

Name	Symbol	Relative atomic mass	Proton number
Iron	Fe	56	
	Pb	207	
Xenon			54
Copper			

Q3 Select from these **elements** to answer the following questions.

iodine, nickel, silicon, sodium, radon, krypton, calcium

a) Which two elements are in the same group? .... and ....

b) Name two elements which are in Period 3. .... and ....

c) Name a transition metal. ....

d) Name a non-metal that is not in Group 0. ....

Q4 Choose from the words below to fill in the blanks in each sentence.

left-hand   right-hand   horizontal   similar   different
vertical   metals   non-metals   increasing   decreasing

a) A group in the periodic table is a .... line of elements.

b) Most of the elements in the periodic table are ....

c) Elements in the periodic table are arranged in order of .... proton number.

d) Non-metals are on the .... side of the periodic table.

e) Elements in the same group have .... properties.

Module C4 — Chemical Patterns

The Periodic Table

Q5 Tick the correct boxes to show whether these statements are **true** or **false**.

True False

a) The rows in the periodic table are also known as periods. ☐ ☐

b) Each **column** in the periodic table contains elements with similar properties. ☐ ☐

c) The periodic table is made up of all the known compounds. ☐ ☐

d) There are more than 70 known elements. ☐ ☐

e) Each new period in the periodic table represents another full shell of electrons. ☐ ☐

Q6 Argon is an extremely **unreactive** gas. Use the periodic table to give the names of two more gases that you would expect to have similar properties to argon.

1. ....

2. ....

Q7 Elements in the same group undergo **similar reactions**.

a) Tick the pairs of elements that would undergo similar reactions.

A potassium and rubidium ☐   C calcium and oxygen ☐

B helium and fluorine ☐   D nitrogen and arsenic ☐

b) Explain how the periodic table shows that fluorine and chlorine would undergo similar reactions.

....

....

Q8 Lithium is **less reactive** than sodium, which is **less reactive** than potassium. Fluorine is **more reactive** than chlorine, which is **more reactive** than bromine. Use this information to choose the correct words in the sentences below.

a) Reactivity **increases** / **decreases** as you go down Group I.

b) Reactivity **increases** / **decreases** as you go down Group VII.

Have a look at the positions of the elements in the periodic table.

Top Tips: The periodic table does more than just tell you the names and symbols of all the elements. You can get some other pretty important information from it too. For starters, it's all arranged in a useful pattern which means that elements with similar properties form columns.

Module C4 — Chemical Patterns

Electron Shells

Q1 a) Tick the boxes to show whether each statement is **true** or **false**.   **True   False**

   i) Electrons occupy shells in atoms.

   ii) The highest energy levels are always filled first.

   iii) Elements in Group 0 have a full outer shell of electrons.

   iv) Reactive elements have full outer shells.

b) Write out corrected versions of the **false** statements.

....

....

....

Q2 Describe **two** things that are wrong with this diagram.

1. ....

....

2. ....

....

Use a periodic table to help you with this question.

Q3 Write out the **electron configurations** for the following elements.

   a) Beryllium   ....   **d)** Calcium   ....

   b) Oxygen   ....   **e)** Aluminium   ....

   c) Silicon   ....   **f)** Argon   ....

Q4 **Chlorine** has an atomic number of 17.

   a) What is its electron configuration?   ....

   b) Draw the electrons on the shells in the diagram.

Module C4 — Chemical Patterns

Group 1 — Alkali Metals

Q1 Sodium, potassium and lithium are all alkali metals.

a) Highlight the location of the alkali metals on this periodic table.

b) Put sodium, potassium and lithium in order of increasing reactivity and state their symbols.

least reactive ....

....

most reactive ....

c) Describe the appearance of the alkali metals.

....

....

Q2 Circle the correct words to complete the passage below.

Sodium is a soft metal with **one** / **two** electron(s) in its outer shell. It reacts vigorously with water, producing **sodium dioxide** / **sodium hydroxide** and **hydrogen** / **oxygen** gas.

Q3 Archibald put a piece of lithium into a beaker of water.

a) Explain why the lithium floated on top of the water.

....

b) After the reaction had finished, Archibald tested the solution to see whether it was acidic, alkaline or neutral. What result would he get?

....

c) Write a **balanced symbol equation** for the reaction.

....

d) i) Write a **word equation** for the reaction between sodium and water.

....

ii) Would you expect the reaction between sodium and water to be **more** or **less** vigorous than the reaction between lithium and water? Explain your answer.

....

Module C4 — Chemical Patterns

Group 7 — Halogens

Q1 Highlight the location of the halogens on this periodic table.

Q2 Draw lines to match each halogen to its correct **symbol**, **description** and **reactivity**.

HALOGEN	SYMBOL	DESCRIPTION	REACTIVITY
bromine	Cl	green gas	most reactive
chlorine	I	grey solid	least reactive
fluorine	Br	red-brown liquid	quite reactive
iodine	F	yellow gas	very reactive

Q3 Decide whether the statements about the halogens below are **true** or **false**.

True False

a) Chlorine gas is made up of molecules which each contain three chlorine atoms. ☐ ☐

b) The halogens can kill bacteria in water. ☐ ☐

c) The halogens become darker in colour as you move down the group. ☐ ☐

d) All the halogens have seven outer electrons. ☐ ☐

Q4 Add the phrases to the table to show how the properties of the halogens change as you go **down** the group.

the melting points of the halogens

the reactivity of the halogens

the boiling points of the halogens

Increase(s) down the group	Decrease(s) down the group

Module C4 — Chemical Patterns

Group 7 — Halogens

Q5 Sodium was reacted with bromine vapour using the equipment shown. White crystals of a new solid were formed during the reaction.

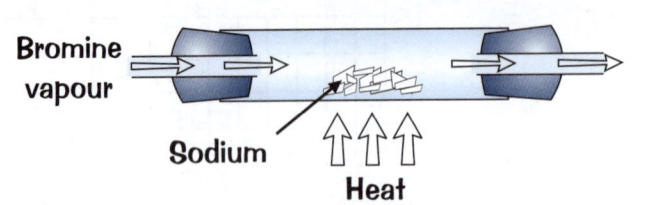

a) Name the white crystals.
   ....

b) Write a **balanced** symbol equation for the reaction.
   ....

c) Would you expect the above reaction to be **faster** or **slower** than a similar reaction between:

   i) sodium and **iodine** vapour? Explain your answer.
   ....

   ii) sodium and **chlorine** vapour? Explain your answer.
   ....

Q6 Equal volumes of **bromine water** were added to two test tubes, each containing a different **potassium halide solution**. The results are shown in the table.

SOLUTION	RESULT
potassium chloride	no colour change
potassium iodide	colour change

a) Explain these results.
   ....
   ....
   ....

b) Write a **balanced symbol equation** for the reaction in the potassium iodide solution.
   ....

c) Would you expect a reaction between:

   i) bromine water and potassium astatide? ....

   ii) bromine water and potassium fluoride? ....

Module C4 — Chemical Patterns

Laboratory Safety

Q1 Fill in the meaning of each hazard symbol by choosing the correct label from the box.

> corrosive   toxic   irritant
> harmful   highly flammable   oxidising

a) ....

b) ....

c) ....

d) ....

e) ....

f) ....

Q2 The **alkali metals** are very reactive and so must be used with great care.

a) Explain why the alkali metals are stored under **oil**.

....

....

b) Suggest what should be done to any apparatus that is going to come into contact with an alkali metal.

....

c) Why must the solutions that the alkali metals form not touch the eyes or the skin?

....

Q3 The **halogens** must also be dealt with very carefully.

a) Why must the halogens only be used inside a fume cupboard?

....

b) Liquid bromine is **corrosive**. Explain what this means.

....

Top Tips: Laboratory safety isn't something that you can afford to skim over. It's important both for your exam and for when you're working in the lab. Unfortunately it's not enough to know that a symbol means that a chemical is dangerous — you need to know how it's dangerous.

Module C4 — Chemical Patterns

Ionic Bonding

Q1 Fill in the gaps in the sentences below by choosing the correct words from the box.

> protons   charged particles   repelled by
> electrons   ions   attracted to   neutral particles

a) In ionic bonding atoms lose or gain .... to form ....

b) Ions are ....

c) Ions with opposite charges are strongly .... each other.

Q2 Use this **diagram** to answer the following questions.

a) How many electrons does **chlorine** need to gain to get a full outer shell of electrons? ....

b) What sort of charge does a **sodium ion** have? ....

c) What is the chemical formula of **sodium chloride**? ....

Q3 Tick the correct boxes to show whether the following statements are **true** or **false**.   True   False

a) Metals generally have fewer electrons in their outer shells than non-metals.

b) Metals tend to form negatively charged ions.

c) Elements in Group 7 gain electrons when they react.

d) Atoms tend to form ions because they are more stable when they have full outer shells.

e) Elements in Group 0 are very reactive.

Q4 Draw a 'dot and cross' diagram to show what happens to the outer shells of electrons when potassium and bromine react.

The diagrams in question 2 are 'dot and cross' diagrams.

Module C4 — Chemical Patterns

Ions and Formulas

Q1 Here are some **elements** and the **ions** they form:

beryllium, Be^{2+} potassium, K^+ iodine, I^- sulfur, S^{2-}

Write down the formulas of four compounds that can be made using just these elements.

1. ....
2. ....
3. ....
4. ....

Make sure the charges on the ions balance.

Q2 Find the charge on the **chloride ion** in calcium chloride.

The formula is $CaCl_2$ and the charge on the calcium ion is 2+.

....

Q3 Use the table to find the **formulas** of the following compounds.

Positive Ions		Negative Ions	
Sodium	Na^+	Chloride	Cl^-
Potassium	K^+	Fluoride	F^-
Calcium	Ca^{2+}	Bromide	Br^-
Iron(II)	Fe^{2+}	Carbonate	CO_3^{2-}
Iron(III)	Fe^{3+}	Sulfate	SO_4^{2-}

a) potassium bromide ....

b) iron(II) chloride ....

c) calcium fluoride ....

Q4 **Aluminium** is in **Group 3** of the periodic table.
Complete the following sentences by choosing the correct word from each pair.

a) An atom of aluminium has **three** / **five** electrons in its outer shell.

b) It will form an ion by **gaining** / **losing** electrons.

c) The charge on an aluminium ion will be **3+** / **3−**.

d) The formula of the compound it makes with chloride ions (Cl^-) will be: **$AlCl_3$** / **Al_3Cl**.

e) The formula of the compound it makes with oxide ions (O^{2-}) will be **Al_2O_3** / **Al_3O_2**.

Module C4 — Chemical Patterns

Chemicals in the Atmosphere

Q1 The table shows some of the **elements** and **compounds** that are found in **dry air**. Complete the table to show whether the substances are elements or compounds, and give the **chemical symbol** or **formula** for each substance.

substance	element or compound?	symbol
oxygen		
carbon dioxide		
argon		
nitrogen		

Q2 Use the words in the box to complete the passage below. Some words can be used more than once.

molecular   compounds   weak   metallic   atoms   non-metallic   strong

Most .... elements and most compounds formed from .... elements are .... substances. The .... within the molecules are held together by very .... covalent bonds. The forces of attraction between the molecules are very ....

Q3 Complete the following sentences by circling the correct option, and **explain** your answers.

a) The melting and boiling points of simple molecular substances are **low / high**.
....

b) Simple molecular substances **conduct / don't conduct** electricity.
....

c) Simple molecular substances are usually **gases and liquids / solids** at room temperature.
....

Q4 The table gives the **melting** and **boiling points** of some **molecular elements**. State whether each will be a **solid**, **liquid** or **gas** at **room temperature** (25 °C).

element	melting point	boiling point
fluorine	−220 °C	−188 °C
bromine	−7 °C	59 °C
iodine	114 °C	185 °C

a) fluorine ....

b) bromine ....

c) iodine ....

Covalent Bonding

Q1 Indicate whether each statement is **true** or **false**.

		True	False
a)	Covalent bonding involves sharing electrons.	☐	☐
b)	Atoms react to gain a full outer shell of electrons.	☐	☐
c)	Some atoms can make both ionic and covalent bonds.	☐	☐
d)	Hydrogen can form two covalent bonds.	☐	☐
e)	Carbon can form four covalent bonds.	☐	☐

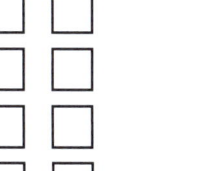

Q2 Complete the following diagrams by adding **electrons**. Only the **outer shells** are shown.

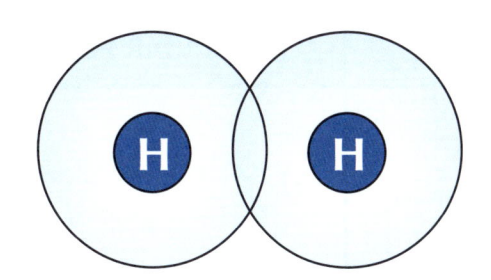

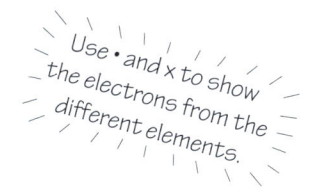

a) Hydrogen (H_2)

Use • and x to show the electrons from the different elements.

b) Carbon dioxide (CO_2)

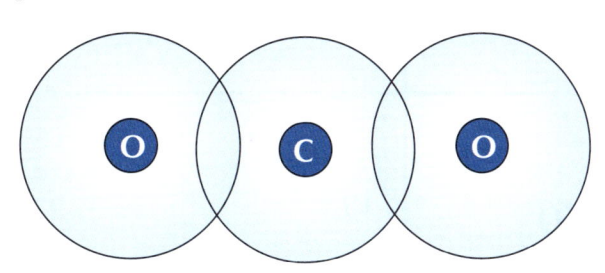

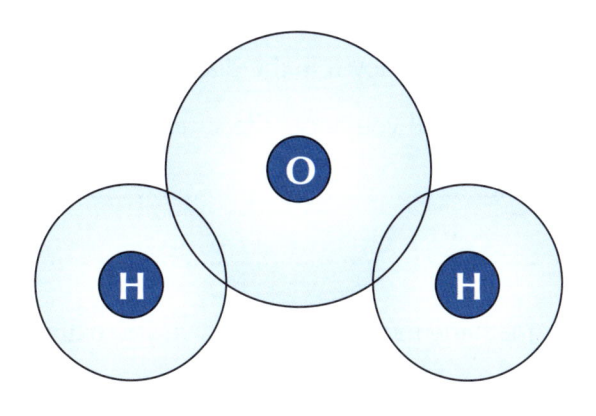

c) Water (H_2O)

Top Tips: Atoms can bond ionically, as you saw back on page 52, or they can bond covalently. Make sure you know what covalent bonds are, and how they arise. It's really important for understanding all about the chemicals that are floating about up there in the atmosphere.

Module C5 — Chemicals of the Natural Environment

Covalent Bonding

Q3 Choose from the words in the box to complete the passage below.

| electronic | positive | electrostatic | neutral | negative |

In a covalent bond, the .... nuclei and the shared .... electrons are held together by .... attraction.

Q4 Complete the table showing the **displayed formulas** and **molecular formulas** of three **carbon compounds**.

DISPLAYED FORMULA	MOLECULAR FORMULA
H—C—H (with H above and below)	a)
b)	NH$_3$
O=S=O	c)

Q5 The **displayed formula** of **methane** is shown in the diagram.

a) What **can't** the displayed formula tell you about the structure of a molecule?

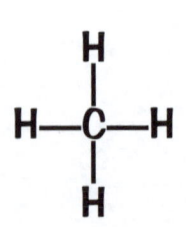

....

....

b) What type of diagram of a methane molecule would give you extra information?

....

Top Tips: There is more than one way of writing a molecule's formula. This isn't just to stop chemists from getting bored — they're all useful for showing different things about the molecule.

Module C5 — Chemicals of the Natural Environment

Chemicals in the Hydrosphere

Q1 Choose from the words in the box to complete the passage below.

| covalent | salty | dissolved | water |
| ionic | salts | gases |

The Earth's hydrosphere consists of all the .... on the Earth's surface and the compounds .... in it. Many of these compounds are ...., and are called .... It is these that make seawater ....

Q2 Potassium chloride is an example of a **salt** found in the **sea**. Mike carries out an experiment to find out if **potassium chloride** conducts electricity. He tests the compound when it's **solid** and when it's **dissolved** in water.

a) Complete the following table of results.

	Conducts electricity?
When solid	
When dissolved in water	

b) Explain your answers to part a).

....

....

....

Q3 Sodium chloride has an **ionic structure**.

a) Circle the correct words to explain why sodium chloride has a high melting point.

Sodium chloride has very **strong** / **weak** chemical bonds between the **negative** / **positive** sodium ions and the **negative** / **positive** chloride ions. This means that it needs a **little** / **large** amount of energy to break the bonds.

b) Name two other **properties** of compounds with **ionic structures**.

1. ....

2. ....

Module C5 — Chemicals of the Natural Environment

Chemicals in the Lithosphere

Q1 Choose from the words in the box to complete the passage describing the Earth's **lithosphere**.

> minerals   aluminium   mantle   silicon
> elements   argon   crust   oxygen

The .... and part of the .... just below it make up the Earth's lithosphere. It mostly consists of a mixture of ...., ..., ... and .... are .... found in large amounts in the crust.

Q2 An **abundant** compound in the Earth's lithosphere is **silicon dioxide**.

a) Give **three** properties of silicon dioxide and explain each in terms of its structure.

Property 1: ....

....

Property 2: ....

....

Property 3: ....

....

b) Give **two** types of rock in which silicon dioxide is found in **large quantities**.

....

Q3 Circle the correct words to complete the following paragraph.

> Giant covalent structures contain **charged ions** / **uncharged atoms**.
> The covalent bonds between the atoms are **strong** / **weak**.
> Giant covalent structures have **high** / **low** melting points, they
> usually **do** / **don't** conduct electricity and they are usually
> **soluble** / **insoluble** in water.

The results suggest a giant covalent structure.

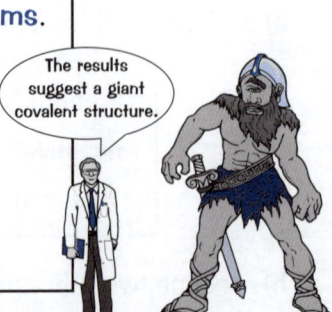

Top Tips: It seems to be all spheres in this section — the atmosphere, the hydrosphere, the lithosphere... Make sure you don't get the facts about them all muddled up. You don't want to be putting the fish up in the sky, or clouds down below the Earth's surface...

Module C5 — Chemicals of the Natural Environment

Chemicals in the Lithosphere

Q4 The tables below show the **percentage composition** of samples of two different types of **rock**.

Decide which sample is **limestone** and which sample is **sandstone**, and explain your answers.

Sample A	% composition
Si	44.0
O	51.0
Al	0.8
Ca	0.7
Mg	0.1
Other	3.4

Sample B	% composition
Si	1.3
O	47.1
Al	1.6
Ca	38.5
C	11.0
Mg	0.5

Sample A is: ....

Reason: ....

Sample B is: ....

Reason: ....

Q5 Some **minerals** are very valuable as **gemstones**.

a) Explain why some minerals are used as gemstones.

....

b) Why are some gemstones so **valuable**?

....

Q6 **Diamond** is a **giant covalent substance** made entirely from **carbon**.

a) Explain why diamond has a **high melting point**.

....

....

b) Explain how diamond's structure makes it **hard**.

....

....

Top Tips: Examiners just love setting data interpretation questions, and this topic is as good as any for finding one. You might have to interpret data about the amounts of elements in different types of rock, or you might have to apply your knowledge of giant covalent structures to other compounds with this type of structure (such as diamond). Don't worry — it's nothing you can't do.

Module C5 — Chemicals of the Natural Environment

Chemicals in the Biosphere

Q1 List **six elements** that all **living things** contain.

1. .... 4. ....
2. .... 5. ....
3. .... 6. ....

Q2 The diagram shows the **structural formula** of a **carbohydrate** molecule. List the **elements** it contains and write its **molecular formula**.

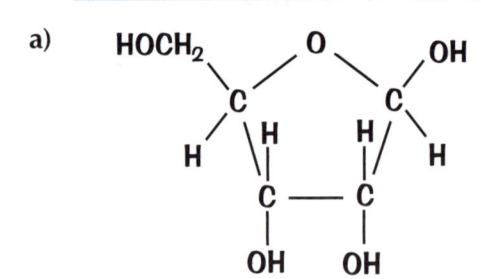

a)

Elements ....

Molecular formula ....

b) In addition to carbon, hydrogen and oxygen, what element do all **protein** molecules contain?

....

Q3 The diagram shows the **nitrogen cycle**.

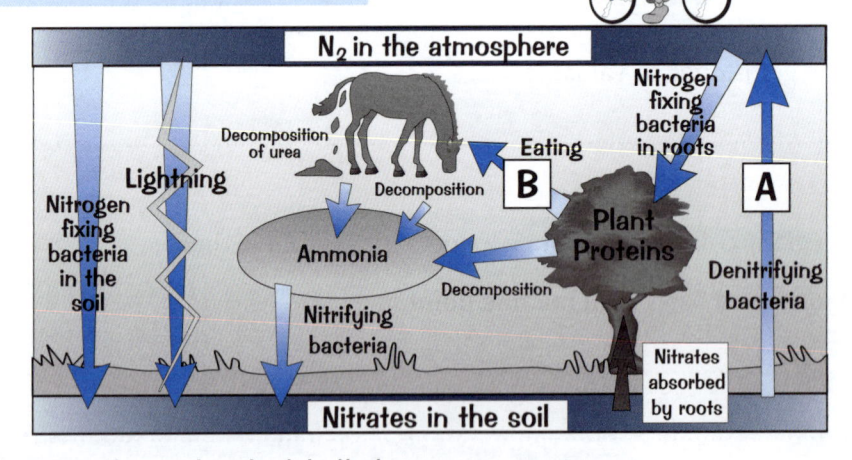

Tick the boxes to show what the labelled arrows represent.

a) Arrow **A** represents:

Denitrifying bacteria moving from the soil to the atmosphere. ☐

Denitrifying bacteria converting nitrates in the soil into nitrogen in the atmosphere. ☐

b) Arrow **B** represents:

Nitrogen from plants moving into animals by feeding. ☐

Nitrogen being released into the atmosphere through feeding. ☐

Module C5 — Chemicals of the Natural Environment

Metals from Minerals

Q1 Indicate whether each of the statements below about **metal ores** is true or false.

                                                                                                True False

    a) Ores are rocks containing minerals from which metals can be extracted.

    b) The more reactive the metal, the easier it is to extract from its ore.

    c) Zinc, iron and copper can all be extracted by heating their ores with carbon monoxide.

    d) When a metal oxide loses oxygen, it is reduced.

Q2 **Copper** may have first been extracted when someone accidentally dropped some copper ore into a **wood fire**. When the ashes were cleared away some copper was left.

    a) Explain how dropping copper ore into a fire could lead to the extraction of copper.

        ....

    b) Why do you think that copper was one of the first metals to be extracted from its ore?

        ....

Q3 Fill in the blanks in the passage below about **extracting metals** from their **ores**.

> .... is often used to extract metals that are
>
> .... it in the reactivity series. Oxygen is removed
>
> from a metal oxide in a process called ....
>
> Other metals have to be extracted using ....
>
> because they are .... reactive.

Q4 Dave is **calculating** how much **metal** can be **extracted** from certain ores.

You'll find a periodic table helpful for these questions.

    a) Calculate the mass of iron that can be extracted from 500 g iron oxide (Fe_2O_3).

        ....

        ....

    b) Could more metal be obtained from the same mass of copper oxide (CuO)?

        ....

        ....

Top Tips: Metals aren't usually found in the ground as pure lumps. They need to be extracted from their ores, and this is done by a variety of methods. The ones you need to know about are reduction using carbon and electrolysis. Which is what these pages are all about...

Module C5 — Chemicals of the Natural Environment

Electrolysis

Q1 Complete the passage about **electrolysis** using words from the box below.

| dissolved | molecules | electric | given to | electrolyte |
| decompose | external circuit | taken from | molten |

During the electrolysis of an ionic compound, an .... current is passed through a .... or .... substance, causing it to ....

Electrons are .... ions at the positive electrode and are passed through the .... to the negative electrode, where they are .... other ions in the solution. Atoms or .... are formed.

Q2 The diagram below shows the electrolysis of **molten aluminium oxide**.

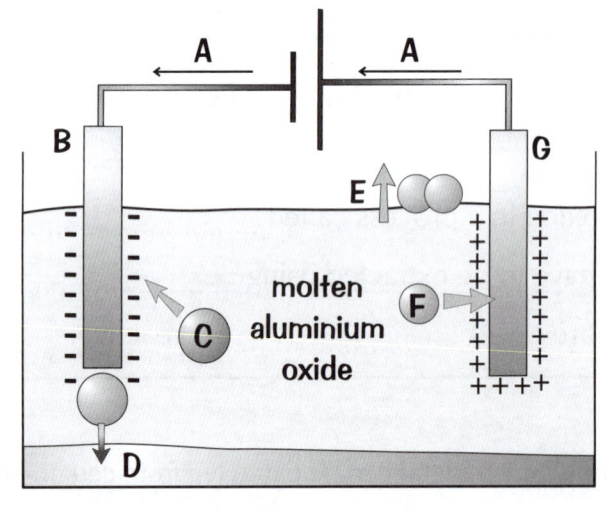

Write the labels that should go at points A–G:

A .... E ....
B .... F ....
C .... G ....
D ....

Q3 Explain why the **electrolyte** needs to be either a **solution** or **molten** for electrolysis to work.

....

....

Module C5 — Chemicals of the Natural Environment

Electrolysis

Q4 a) Tick the correct boxes to show whether the following statements are **true** or **false**.

       True   False

i) Ionic substances can only be electrolysed if molten or in solution.

ii) In the extraction of aluminium the electrolyte is molten aluminium metal.

iii) The aluminium produced is molten.

iv) Aluminium ions gain electrons in electrolysis.

v) Aluminium is formed at the positive electrode.

b) Write out a correct version of each false statement.

....

....

....

....

Q5 **Aluminium** is the most **abundant** metal in the Earth's crust.

  a) **i)** Circle the correct word:

        The most common aluminium ore is bauxite / cryolite.

      ii) When this ore is mined and purified, which compound is obtained? Give its name and formula.

        Name .... **Formula** ....

  b) Why can't aluminium be extracted by **reduction** with carbon?

....

  c) Although it's very common, aluminium was not discovered until about 200 years ago. Suggest why.

....

Q6 **Aluminium** is extracted from its ore by **electrolysis**.

Write balanced half-equations for the reactions at the electrodes.

Negative electrode: ....

Positive electrode: ....

Top Tips: Usually, things that are common are cheap to buy — like potatoes. But, even though aluminium is as common a metal as you're going to get, it's not actually that cheap because it costs a lot to extract. (Potatoes, on the other hand, are easy to extract — just get digging.)

Module C5 — Chemicals of the Natural Environment

Metals

Q1 The table shows the **properties** of **four elements** found in the periodic table.

ELEMENT	MELTING POINT (°C)	DENSITY (g/cm^3)	ELECTRICAL CONDUCTIVITY
A	1084	8.9	Excellent
B	−39	13.6	Very good
C	3500	3.51	Very poor
D	1536	7.87	Very good

a) Which **three** of the above elements are most likely to be **metals**?

....

b) Explain how you know the other element is **not** a metal.

....

....

Q2 This table shows some of the **properties** of four different **metals**.

Metal	Heat conduction	Cost	Resistance to corrosion	Strength
1	average	high	excellent	good
2	average	medium	good	excellent
3	excellent	low	good	good
4	low	high	average	poor

Use the information in the table to choose which metal would be **best** for making:

a) Saucepan bases ....

b) Car bodies ....

c) A statue for a town centre ....

Think about how long a statue would have to last for.

Q3 Complete the following sentences about metals.

a) Metals have a giant .... structure.

b) Metals are good conductors of .... and ....

c) The atoms in metals can slide over each other, so metals are ....

Module C5 — Chemicals of the Natural Environment

Metals

Q4 All metals have a similar **structure**. This explains why many of them have similar **properties**.

a) Draw a labelled diagram of a typical metal structure, showing the electrons.

b) What is unusual about the electrons in a metal?

....

Q5 Complete the following sentences by choosing from the words in the box.

Each word should only be used once (or not at all).

| hammered | weak | low | high | strong | malleable | folded |

a) Metals have a .... tensile strength.

b) Metals are .... and hard to break.

c) Metals can be .... into different shapes because they are ....

Q6 Explain how **electricity** is conducted through metals.

....

....

Q7 Explain why most metals have **high melting points**.

....

....

Top Tip: Okay, so metals form weird bonds. The electrons can go wandering about through the material, and it's this that gives them some of their characteristic properties. It's pretty important that you learn the key phrases that examiners like — 'giant structure', 'sea of free electrons', etc.

Module C5 — Chemicals of the Natural Environment

Environmental Impact

Q1 Ores are **finite resources**.

a) Explain what finite resources are.

....

....

b) Explain why it is a **problem** that ores are finite resources.
Suggest one thing that can be done to **reduce** this problem.

....

....

Q2 New **mines** always have **social**, **economic** and **environmental** consequences. Complete this table by putting **two** more effects that a new mine can have in each of the columns.

Remember to include both positive and negative effects.

Social	Economic	Environmental
Services, e.g. Healthcare may be improved because of influx of people.		Pollution from traffic.

Top Tips: It's important to be able to weigh up the issues surrounding the extraction of metals. There are plenty of positive and negative effects of mining, so make sure you've got them sorted here so that you don't have to spend loads of time thinking if they come up in the exam.

Module C5 — Chemicals of the Natural Environment

Environmental Impact

Q3 Read the article below and answer the questions that follow.

Metals play a major role in modern life. However, none of the stages in the life cycle of a metal product are free from environmental problems.

Mining
Although mining brings money and employment, which have a positive impact on the development of an area, there are plenty of negatives. Mining destroys landscapes and habitats, produces waste products and causes noise pollution. Transporting the ore takes energy and causes pollution.

Extraction
Extracting pure metal from the ore is also not without problems. Non-renewable resources, such as fossil fuels, are usually used to provide the energy needed to extract the metals. This in turn leads to air pollution, which has its own problems such as acid rain and climate change.

Use
Metals are often used for products which have an impact on the environment. Take, for example, cars — they burn non-renewable fuels and produce pollution.

Disposal
At the end of their life, metals are often disposed of in landfill sites. These are unattractive and some metals can be dangerous if disposed of in this way. Vehicles accessing the sites cause pollution, dust and noise.

One answer to these problems is recycling. Take aluminium — it can be recycled over and over again without losing any of its properties in the process. The process doesn't take long either — recycled aluminium cans are usually back on the shelves within eight weeks.

In the UK, it's estimated that we use about 5 billion aluminium cans every year. In 2001, 42% of these cans were recycled (up from 31% of cans used in 1996).

Recycling aluminium uses only 5% of the energy needed to extract pure aluminium from bauxite, and produces only 5% of the carbon dioxide emissions.

For every 1 kg of aluminium recycled, 6 kg of bauxite, 4 kg of chemical products and 14 kWh of electricity are saved. Put another way, 20 recycled cans can be made with the energy it takes to make just one brand new can.

The use of aluminium is rising quickly so it makes sense to encourage people to recycle more aluminium. However, not all areas have good recycling collection services, and some people don't make the effort to separate their recyclable waste. Some people also wonder whether it is 'environmentally friendly' to produce all the plastic boxes used to collect cans from doorsteps.

Module C5 — Chemicals of the Natural Environment

Environmental Impact

a) Give two **environmental problems** associated with the mining of metal ores.
....
....

b) Describe one **benefit** that an aluminium ore mine can have for the local area.
....

c) How can the use of metals cause environmental problems **indirectly**?
....

d) Suggest why it is a good thing that aluminium does not lose its properties during the recycling process.
....

e) By how much did the percentage of aluminium cans recycled increase between **1996** and **2001**?
....

f) The article states that about 5 billion aluminium cans are used every year in the UK. How many cans were **recycled** in **2001**?
....

g) State **two** reasons that people might give for not recycling their aluminium packaging.
....
....

h) Select one sentence or phrase from the article that demonstrates that recycling aluminium is very energy efficient.
....
....

i) Give **one** problem that could be associated with the use of kerbside recycling boxes.
....
....

Module C5 — Chemicals of the Natural Environment

Module C6 — Chemical Synthesis

Industrial Chemical Synthesis

Q1 Explain what is meant by **chemical synthesis**.

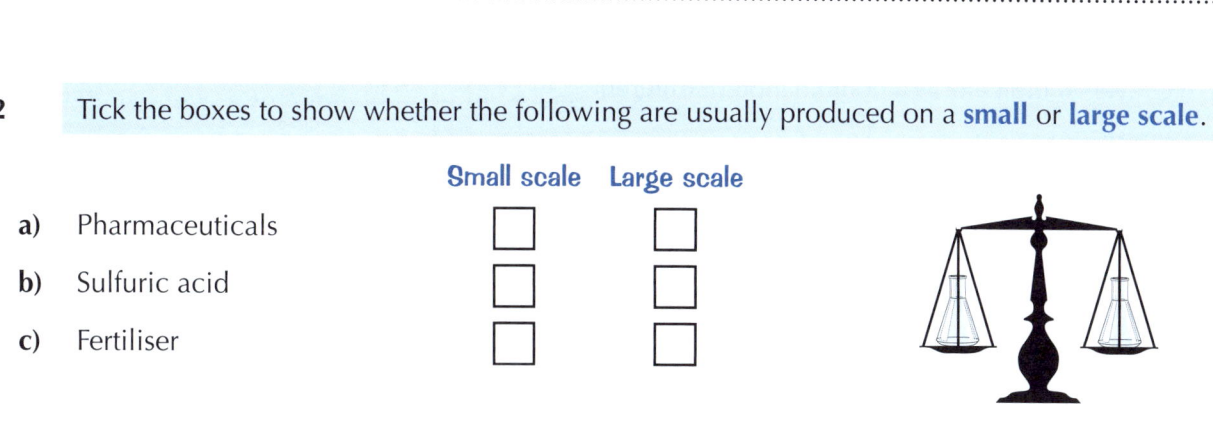

....

Q2 Tick the boxes to show whether the following are usually produced on a **small** or **large scale**.

	Small scale	Large scale
a) Pharmaceuticals	☐	☐
b) Sulfuric acid	☐	☐
c) Fertiliser	☐	☐

Q3 Modern industry uses thousands of tonnes of **sulfuric acid** per day. The pie chart shows the major **uses** of the sulfuric acid produced by a particular plant.

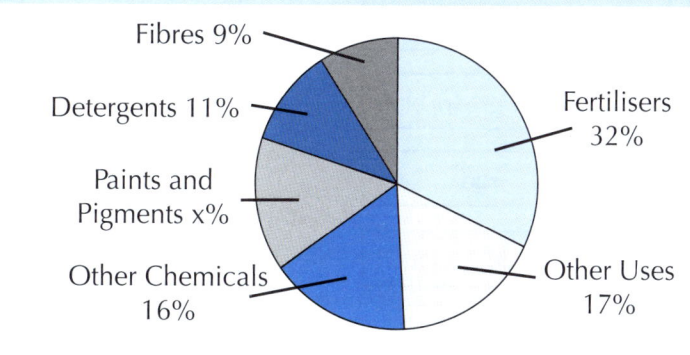

Fibres 9%
Detergents 11%
Paints and Pigments x%
Other Chemicals 16%
Fertilisers 32%
Other Uses 17%

a) What is the **main use** of the sulfuric acid from this plant?

....

b) What percentage of the sulfuric acid from this plant is used in the production of paints and pigments?

....

Q4 The bar chart shows the number of people **employed** in various sectors of the **chemical industry** in country X.

a) Which **sector** employs the **most** people?

....

b) How many people **in total** are employed in the chemical industry in country X?

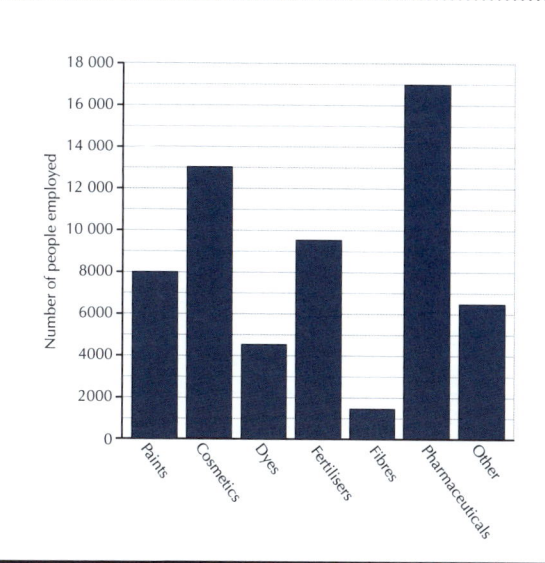

....

Module C6 — Chemical Synthesis

Acids and Alkalis

Q1 Complete each of the following sentences with a single word.

a) Solutions which are not acidic or alkaline are said to be ....

b) A neutral substance has a pH of ....

c) Universal indicator is a combination of different ....

d) An alkali is a substance with a pH of .... than 7.

Q2 Draw lines to match the substances and their universal indicator colours to their **pH** values and **acid/alkali strengths**.

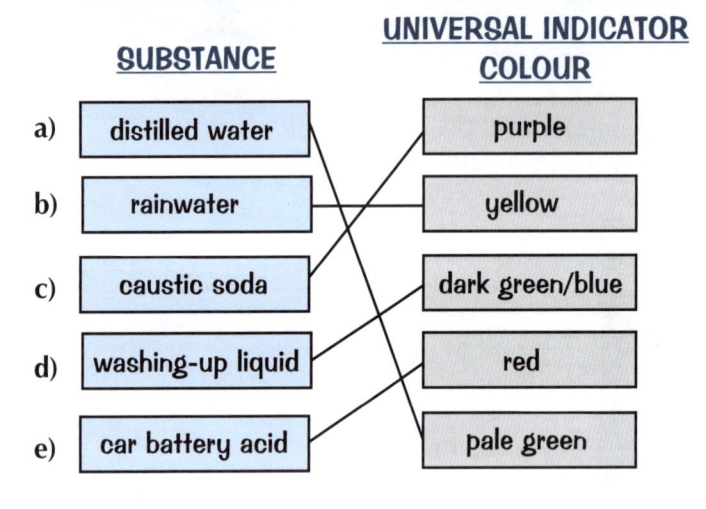

SUBSTANCE	UNIVERSAL INDICATOR COLOUR	pH	ACID/ALKALI STRENGTH
a) distilled water	purple	5/6	strong alkali
b) rainwater	yellow	8/9	weak alkali
c) caustic soda	dark green/blue	14	weak acid
d) washing-up liquid	red	7	neutral
e) car battery acid	pale green	1	strong acid

Q3 Many chemicals that people use **every day** are **acids** or **alkalis**.

a) Complete the following passage using words from the box.

| hydrogen chloride | solids | more | tartaric | ethanoic | less | liquid | nitric |

Acids are substances with a pH of .... than 7.

Pure acidic compounds are found in various different states, for example citric acid and .... acid are both ....

Sulfuric acid is an example of a .... acidic compound, as are .... and .... acids.

There are also acidic compounds that are gases — .... is one example.

b) Name three common **alkalis** that are **hydroxides**.

....

Module C6 — Chemical Synthesis

Acids and Alkalis

Q4 Indigestion is caused by too much acid in the stomach.
Antacid tablets contain alkalis, which neutralise the excess acid.

a) Which is the correct word equation for a **neutralisation reaction**? Circle the correct answer.

salt + acid → alkali + water   acid + alkali → salt + water   acid + water → alkali + salt

b) Say what is produced when:

i) an acidic compound is dissolved in water.

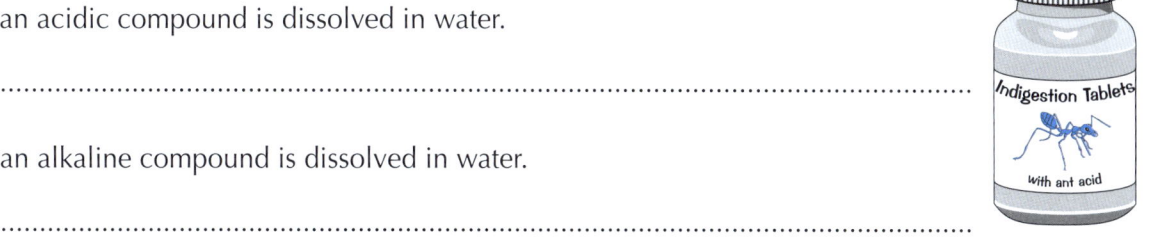

....

ii) an alkaline compound is dissolved in water.

....

Joey wanted to test whether some antacid tablets really did **neutralise acid**. He added a tablet to some hydrochloric acid, stirred it until it dissolved and tested the pH of the solution. Further tests were carried out after dissolving a second, third and fourth tablet.
His results are shown in the table below.

Tablets added	pH of acid
0	1
1	2
2	3
3	7
4	7

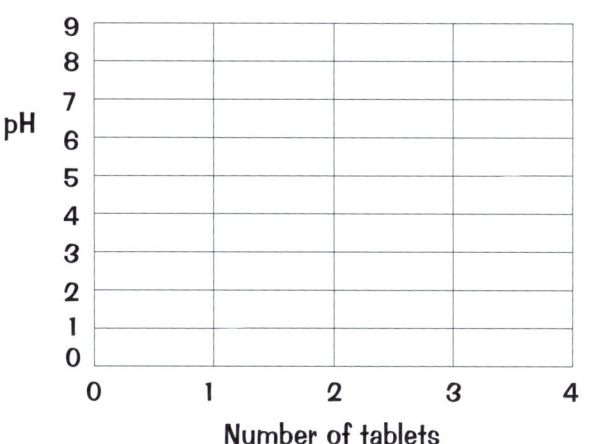

c) i) Plot a graph of the results on the grid shown.

ii) How many tablets were needed to neutralise the acid? ....

d) Give two ways Joey could have tested the pH of the solution.

1. ....

2. ....

Q5 When an acid and an alkali react the products are **neutral**. This is called a **neutralisation** reaction.

a) Describe what happens to the **hydrogen ions** from the acid and the **hydroxide ions** from the alkali during a neutralisation reaction.

....

b) Write a balanced symbol equation to illustrate the reaction between the **hydrogen ions** from the acid and the **hydroxide ions** from the alkali during a neutralisation reaction.

....

Module C6 — Chemical Synthesis

Acids Reacting with Metals

Q1 The diagram below shows **magnesium** reacting with **hydrochloric acid**.

a) Label the diagram with the names of the chemicals.

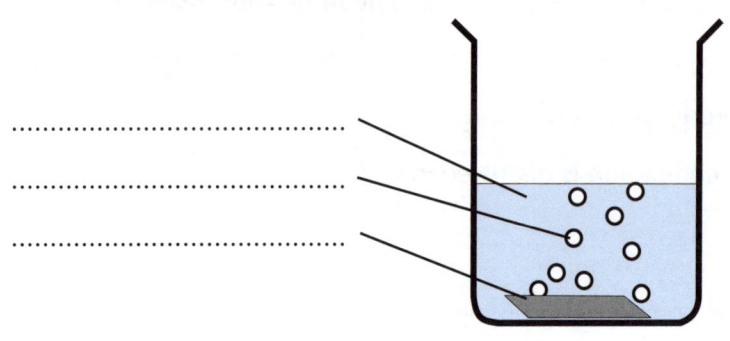

b) Complete the word equation for this reaction:

magnesium + ... → **magnesium chloride** + ...

c) Write a **balanced** symbol equation for the reaction.

....

The formula of magnesium chloride is MgCl.

d) All metals will react with acids in a similar way.
Zinc reacts with sulfuric acid. Give the **word** equation for this reaction.

....

Q2 Write out **balanced** symbol equations for the following reactions. Include **state symbols**.

a) calcium + hydrochloric acid

....

b) zinc + hydrochloric acid

....

c) magnesium + sulfuric acid

....

d) **Hydrobromic acid** reacts with **magnesium** to form a bromide salt and hydrogen, as shown in the equation below.

$$Mg(s) + 2HBr(l) \rightarrow MgBr_2(aq) + H_2(g)$$

Write a balanced symbol equation for the reaction between **aluminium** and hydrobromic acid. (The formula of aluminium bromide is $AlBr_3$.)

....

Module C6 — Chemical Synthesis

Oxides, Hydroxides and Carbonates

Q1 Give the **general word equation** for the reaction between an **acid** and:

a) a metal oxide ....

b) a metal carbonate ....

c) a metal hydroxide ....

Q2 Fill in the blanks to complete the word equations for **acids** reacting with **metal oxides** and **metal hydroxides**.

a) hydrochloric acid + lead oxide → .... chloride + water

b) nitric acid + copper hydroxide → copper .... + water

c) sulfuric acid + zinc oxide → zinc sulfate + ...

d) hydrochloric acid + ... oxide → nickel .... + ...

e) .... acid + copper oxide → .... nitrate + ...

f) sulfuric acid + ... hydroxide → sodium .... + ...

A metal-ox-hide

Q3 Complete the following symbol equations for **acids** reacting with **metal carbonates**.

a) $2HNO_3(l) + Na_2CO_3(s) \rightarrow$ .... + ... + ...

b) $H_2SO_4(l) +$ .... $\rightarrow MgSO_4(aq) +$ .... + ...

Q4 Write symbol equations for the following reactions.

a) sulfuric acid + copper oxide

....

The formula of copper oxide is CuO.

b) nitric acid + magnesium oxide

....

c) sulfuric acid + sodium hydroxide

....

Top Tips: At first glance it looks quite scary, all this writing equations — but it's not that bad, honest. The key is to learn the basic rules inside out. Once you've got them mastered it's really just a case of swapping a few bits round and filling in the gaps. No reason to panic at all.

Module C6 — Chemical Synthesis

Oxides, Hydroxides and Carbonates

Q5 **Acids** react with **metal carbonates** in neutralisation reactions. Write **balanced symbol equations** for the following reactions.

a) hydrochloric acid + copper carbonate

....

The formula of copper carbonate is CuCO₃.

b) nitric acid + magnesium carbonate

....

c) sulfuric acid + lithium carbonate

....

The formula of lithium carbonate is LiCO₃.

d) hydrochloric acid + calcium carbonate

....

e) sulfuric acid + sodium carbonate

....

Q6 Amir was investigating how he could restore a tarnished copper ornament. He obtained some **copper compounds** and looked at the effect of reacting them with dilute **hydrochloric acid** (HCl).

SUBSTANCE TESTED	FORMULA	COLOUR	OBSERVATIONS WHEN ADDED TO THE ACID
copper carbonate	CuCO₃	green	fizzed and dissolved forming a blue solution
copper hydroxide	Cu(OH)₂	blue	dissolved slowly forming a blue solution
copper oxide	CuO	black	dissolved very slowly forming a blue solution

a) i) Why does copper carbonate fizz when it reacts with an acid?

....

ii) Write a word equation for the reaction between hydrochloric acid and copper carbonate.

....

b) Amir tested part of the copper ornament with the acid and it fizzed. Which compound is likely to be present on the surface of the ornament?

....

c) Write a balanced symbol equation for the reaction of hydrochloric acid with copper hydroxide.

....

Module C6 — Chemical Synthesis

Synthesising Compounds

Q1 Draw lines to match each description to the type of reaction it is describing.

- an acid and an alkali react to produce a salt — precipitation
- a compound breaks down on heating — neutralisation
- an insoluble solid forms when two solutions are mixed — thermal decomposition

Q2 In the synthesis of any **organic chemical** there are a number of **important stages**.

a) Complete the passage using words from the box below.

| harmed | reduce | hazards | injury | action |

A risk assessment should identify any stage in the process that could cause .... This usually involves identifying .... and the people who might be .... Risk assessments also include what .... can be taken to .... the risk.

b) When making a chemical on an industrial scale it is often important to calculate accurately the quantities of reactants to be used. Explain why.

....
....

c) Give **two** factors that should be considered when choosing the apparatus in which a reaction will be carried out.

....
....

Q3 Explain why each of the following might be carried out during chemical synthesis.

a) Filtration

....

b) Evaporation

....

c) Drying

....

Module C6 — Chemical Synthesis

Synthesising Compounds

Q4 Read the article below and answer the questions that follow.

Sodium Bromide

To most people sodium bromide looks like any other white, crystalline salt. What people don't realise is the vast number of uses it has in the chemical industry, ranging from photography to pharmaceuticals. As with most inorganic chemicals, there are a number of different stages in the production of sodium bromide.

Industrial Synthesis

Sodium bromide (NaBr) is usually produced by reacting sodium hydroxide (NaOH) with hydrobromic acid (HBr):

Sodium hydroxide + hydrobromic acid → sodium bromide + water

Although this is a relatively simple reaction, the plant used to produce sodium bromide is quite high-tech. Sodium hydroxide is highly reactive so it's important to use the right equipment. The reaction vessel must be able to withstand the corrosive effects of sodium hydroxide and the large amount of heat produced when it reacts with hydrobromic acid.

The production of sodium bromide doesn't involve a catalyst, so the main way to control the rate of reaction is to alter the concentrations of the reactants.

After reacting sodium hydroxide with hydrobromic acid, the sodium bromide is extracted by evaporation — this involves heating the sodium bromide solution. The water is evaporated, leaving behind white crystals of sodium bromide. After the product has been isolated it is then purified.

Yield and purity

The yield of sodium bromide produced is then calculated. For financial reasons it's important to produce a high yield, so chemical engineers are always looking for ways to modify the process to give a higher yield. The purity of the product is also calculated at this stage.

Safety

People working on sodium bromide production need to take a number of safety precautions. This is because of the highly corrosive and reactive nature of the sodium hydroxide. Sodium bromide also has its risks — it's harmful if swallowed and can irritate the skin and eyes.

Uses of sodium bromide

Sodium bromide has a range of different uses in the chemical industry. The data on the right is from a large chemical company that supplies sodium bromide to different sectors in the chemical industry. It shows what the sodium bromide it produces is used for.

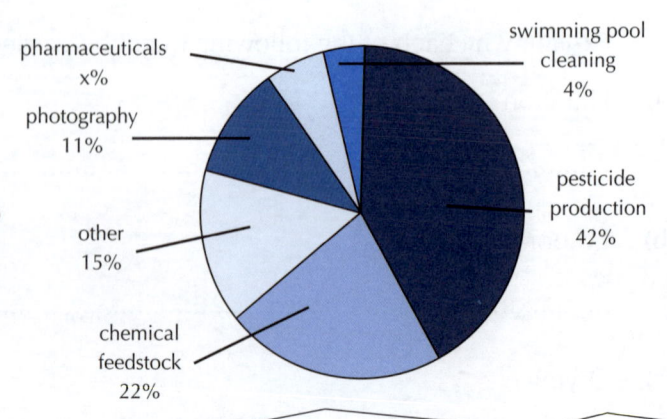

- pharmaceuticals x%
- photography 11%
- other 15%
- chemical feedstock 22%
- swimming pool cleaning 4%
- pesticide production 42%

Module C6 — Chemical Synthesis

Synthesising Compounds

a) i) What **type** of reaction is used to produce sodium bromide?

    ....

    ii) Write a balanced symbol equation (including state symbols) to show the formation of sodium bromide.

    ....

b) Give **two** reasons why it is important to choose a suitable reaction vessel for the production of sodium bromide.

    ....

    ....

c) Suggest why **evaporation** is used to separate the sodium bromide from the reaction mixture.

    ....

d) Suggest a method that could be used to **purify** the sodium bromide.

    ....

e) The article describes how sodium hydroxide and sodium bromide are dangerous.

    i) When planning the synthesis of any compound, what is the process of identifying possible hazards called?

    ....

    ii) Give two hazards associated with **sodium bromide**.

    ....

    ....

f) Why is it useful to calculate the **yield** of sodium bromide?

    ....

g) i) Which industry does the company in the article supply the most sodium bromide to?

    ....

    ii) What percentage of their sodium bromide is used in the pharmaceutical industry?

    ....

    iii) If the company produces 3000 tonnes of sodium bromide per year, what **mass** is used in photography?

    ....

Module C6 — Chemical Synthesis

Relative Formula Mass

Q1 All elements have a relative atomic mass, A_r.

   a) Complete the following sentence by filling in the blanks.

   > The relative atomic mass of an element shows the .... of its atoms relative to the mass of one .... of ....

   b) Give the **relative atomic masses** (A_r) of the following elements. Use the periodic table to help you.

   i) magnesium ....   iv) hydrogen ....   vii) K ....
   ii) neon ....   v) C ....   viii) Ca ....
   iii) oxygen ....   vi) Cu ....   ix) Cl ....

Q2 Use the periodic table to identify the elements A, B and C.

   > Element A has an A_r of 4.
   > Element B has an A_r 3 times that of element A.
   > Element C has an A_r 4 times that of element A.

   Element A = ...
   Element B = ...
   Element C = ...

Q3 a) Explain how the **relative formula mass** of a **compound** is calculated.

   ....

   b) Give the **relative formula masses** (M_r) of the following:

   i) water, H_2O ....

   ii) potassium chloride, KOH ....

   iii) nitric acid, HNO_3 ....

   iv) magnesium hydroxide, $Mg(OH)_2$ ....

   v) iron(III) hydroxide, $Fe(OH)_3$ ....

Top Tips: The periodic table really comes in useful here. There's no way you'll be able to answer these questions without one (unless you've memorised all the elements' relative atomic masses — and that would just be silly). And luckily for you, you'll be given one in your exam. Yay!

Module C6 — Chemical Synthesis

Calculating Masses in Reactions

Q1 Anna burns **10 g** of **magnesium** in air to produce **magnesium oxide** (MgO).

   a) Write out the **balanced equation** for this reaction.

   ....

   b) Calculate the mass of **magnesium oxide** that's produced.

   ....

   ....

   ....

Q2 What mass of **sodium** is needed to make **2 g** of **sodium oxide**?

$$4Na + O_2 \rightarrow 2Na_2O$$

....

....

....

Q3 **Aluminium** and **iron oxide** (Fe_2O_3) react together to produce **aluminium oxide** (Al_2O_3) and **iron**.

   a) Write out the **balanced equation** for this reaction.

   ....

   b) What **mass** of iron is produced from **20 g** of iron oxide?

   ....

   ....

   ....

Q4 When heated, **limestone** ($CaCO_3$) decomposes to form **calcium oxide** (CaO) and **carbon dioxide**.

   How many **kilograms** of limestone are needed to make **100 kilograms** of **calcium oxide**?

   The calculation is exactly the same — just use 'kg' instead of 'g'.

   ....

   ....

   ....

Module C6 — Chemical Synthesis

Calculating Masses in Reactions

Q5 **Iron oxide** is reduced to **iron** inside a blast furnace using carbon. There are **three** stages involved.

Stage A $C + O_2 \rightarrow CO_2$

Stage B $CO_2 + C \rightarrow 2CO$

Stage C $3CO + Fe_2O_3 \rightarrow 2Fe + 3CO_2$

If **10 g** of **carbon** are used in stage B, and all the carbon monoxide produced gets used in stage C, what **mass** of CO_2 is produced in **stage C**?

....

....

Work out the mass of CO at the end of stage B first.

....

....

Q6 **Sodium sulfate** (Na_2SO_4) is made by reacting **sodium hydroxide** (NaOH) with **sulfuric acid** (H_2SO_4). **Water** is also produced.

a) Write out the **balanced equation** for this reaction.

....

b) What mass of **sodium hydroxide** is needed to make **75 g** of **sodium sulfate**?

....

....

....

....

c) What mass of **water** is formed when **50 g** of **sulfuric acid** reacts?

....

....

....

....

Module C6 — Chemical Synthesis

Isolating the Product and Measuring Yield

Q1 James wanted to produce **silver chloride** (AgCl). He added a carefully measured mass of silver nitrate to some dilute hydrochloric acid. An **insoluble white solid** formed.

a) Complete the formula for calculating percentage yield, and its labels, using words from the box. Words can be used more than once.

| reactants | weighing | theoretical yield | pure | dried | actual yield | maximum |

This is the mass of pure dry product. It is found by .... the dried product.

$$\text{percentage yield} = \frac{\text{..................................}}{\text{..................................}} \times 100$$

This is the .... of the product as a percentage of the ....

This is the .... amount of ...., dried product that could have been made using the amounts of .... you started with.

b) James calculated that he should get 2.7 g of silver chloride, but he only got 1.2 g. What was the **percentage yield**?

....

c) What **method** should James use to separate silver chloride from the solution?

....

Silver chloride is an insoluble solid.

d) James left the silver chloride to dry on the bench. Suggest two ways the product could have been dried if the reaction was being carried out on a large scale.

1. ....

2. ....

Q2 Emilio and Julio need to separate a **soluble solid** from a **solution**.

a) Suggest a method they could use to separate the soluble solid from solution.

....

b) How can the method you suggested in part a) be useful when purifying a product?

....

Module C6 — Chemical Synthesis

Titrations

Q1 Titrations are used widely in industry, for example when determining the **purity** of a substance.

a) If a solid product is being tested why must it first be made into a **solution**?

....

b) Fill in the blanks using words from the box below to describe how a solution is made and draw lines to connect each statement to the diagram it describes. You can use the words more than once.

| solvent | weigh | swirl | dissolved | crush | water | titration |

① .... the solid product into a powder.

② .... some of the powdered product into a .... flask.

③ The powder is then .... by adding some .... (e.g. ....).

④ .... the flask until all of the solid has ....

c) Label the following pieces of apparatus used in a titration experiment.

....

....

d) Describe how you would carry out a titration.

....

....

....

Module C6 — Chemical Synthesis

Purity

Q1 Pharmaceutical companies need to ensure that the drugs they produce are pure.

a) Give two methods that can be used to improve the purity of a product.

1. .... 2. ....

b) Why is it important to control the purity of chemicals such as pharmaceuticals?

....

....

Q2 Ruth works in the quality assurance department of a company that produces fizzy drinks. The drinks contain citric acid. One of Ruth's jobs is to test the purity of the citric acid before it is used to make the drinks. She does this by carrying out an acid-alkali titration.

a) What type of reaction do titrations involve? Circle the correct answer.

　　　precipitation　　　　　　esterification　　　　　　neutralisation

b) Ruth starts off with **0.3 g of citric acid** dissolved in **25 cm³** of water. When she carries out the titration she finds that it takes **21.6 cm³ of 2.5 g/dm³ sodium hydroxide** (NaOH) to neutralise the citric acid. Calculate the purity of the citric acid by completing the following steps.

i) Calculate the **concentration** of the citric acid solution using the equation:

$$\text{conc. of citric acid solution} = 4.8 \times \frac{\text{conc. of NaOH} \times \text{vol. of NaOH}}{\text{vol. of citric acid solution}}$$

....

....

ii) Calculate the **mass** of the citric acid using the equation:

$$\text{mass of citric acid} = \text{concentration of citric acid} \times \text{volume}$$

....

iii) Calculate the **percentage purity** of the citric acid using the equation:

$$\% \text{ purity} = \frac{\text{calculated mass of citric acid}}{\text{mass of citric acid at start}} \times 100\%$$

....

....

Module C6 — Chemical Synthesis

Rates of Reaction

Q1 a) Match these common chemical reactions to the **speed** at which they happen.

- a firework exploding
- hair being dyed
- an apple rotting

- SLOW (hours or longer)
- MODERATE SPEED (minutes)
- FAST (seconds or shorter)

- a match burning
- a ship rusting

b) Explain what is meant by the term 'rate of chemical reaction'.

....

....

Q2 When chemicals are produced on an **industrial scale** it is important to control the **rates of reactions**.

Complete the passage below using words from the box.

> explosion   economic   costs   fast   safety   optimum   yield   compromise

The rates of reactions in industrial chemical synthesis need to be controlled for two main reasons. Firstly for .... reasons. If the reaction is too .... it could cause an ...., which may injure or even kill employees. Chemical reactions are also controlled for .... reasons. Companies usually choose .... conditions. These will usually involve a .... between the ...., rate of reaction and production ....

Q3 The graph shows the results from an experiment using **magnesium** and dilute **hydrochloric acid**. The **volume of gas** produced was measured at regular intervals as the reaction proceeded.

a) Which reaction was **faster**, P or Q?

....

b) Which reaction produced the **largest volume of gas**, P, Q or R?

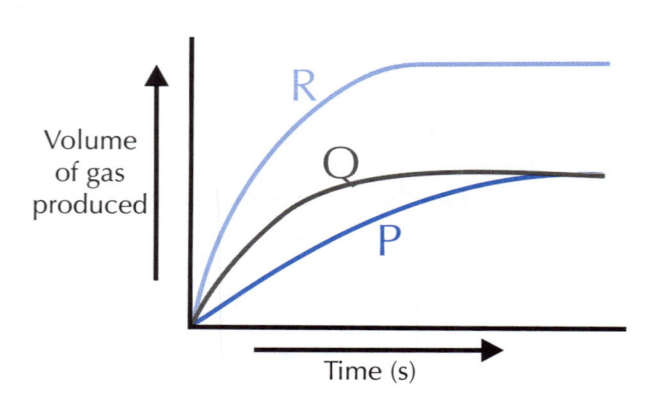

....

c) On the curve for reaction R, mark with an **X** the point where the reaction finishes.

Module C6 — Chemical Synthesis

Rates of Reaction

Q4 Circle the correct words to complete the sentences below.

a) The **higher** / lower the temperature, the faster the rate of reaction.

b) A higher / **lower** concentration will reduce the rate of reaction.

c) A smaller particle size **increases** / decreases the rate of reaction.

d) Using a catalyst **increases** / decreases the rate of reaction.

Nora's reactions were slow in the cold.

Q5 In an experiment to investigate **reaction rates**, strips of **magnesium** were put into tubes containing different concentrations of **hydrochloric acid**. The time taken for the magnesium to 'disappear' was measured. The results are shown in the table.

Conc. of acid (mol/dm^3)	Time taken (seconds)
0.01	298
0.02	147
0.04	74
0.08	37
0.10	30
0.20	15

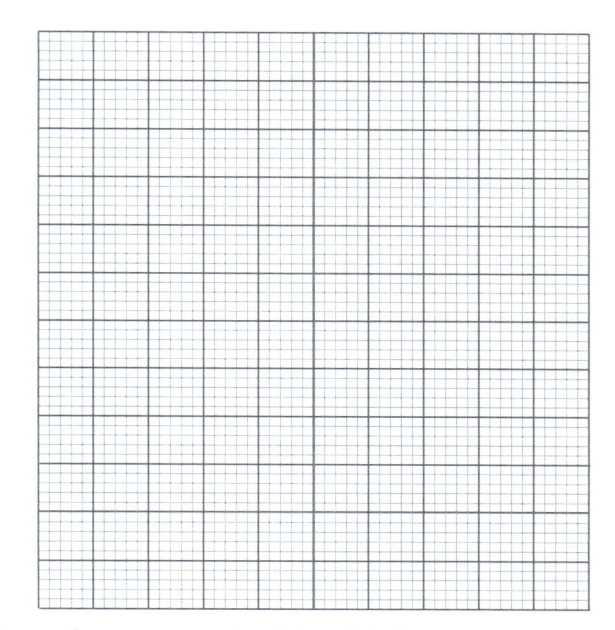

a) Give **three** things that should be kept the same in each case to make this a **fair test**.

....

....

b) Plot a graph of the data on the grid provided, with concentration of acid on the horizontal axis and time on the vertical axis.

c) What do the results tell you about how the concentration of acid affects the rate of the reaction?

....

d) Would the rates of the reaction have been different if magnesium powder had been used instead? If so, how?

....

....

Top Tips: It's a pretty good idea to learn the four things that reaction rate depends on (temperature, concentration, surface area and using a catalyst). It's an even better idea to learn exactly how these four things affect the rate of a reaction and what happens when you change them.

Module C6 — Chemical Synthesis

Collision Theory

Q1 Complete the following passage by circling the correct word(s) from each pair.

> In order for a reaction to occur, the particles must **remain still** / **collide**. If you heat up a reaction mixture, you give the particles more **energy** / **surface area**. This makes them move **faster** / **more slowly** and so there is **more** / **less** chance of successful collisions. So, increasing the temperature increases the **concentration** / **rate of reaction**.

Q2 Reactions involving solutions are affected by the **concentration**.

a) If you increase the concentration of a solution, does the rate of reaction **increase** or **decrease**? Explain your answer.

....

....

b) In the boxes on the right, draw two diagrams, one showing a solution containing two different types of particle at low concentration, the other showing a high concentration of the solution.

low concentration   high concentration

Q3 Here are five statements about **surface area** and rates of reaction. Tick the appropriate box to show whether each is **true** or **false**.

True   False

a) Breaking a solid into smaller pieces decreases its surface area. ☐ ☐

b) A larger surface area will mean a faster rate of reaction. ☐ ☐

c) A larger surface area decreases the number of useful collisions. ☐ ☐

d) Powdered marble has a larger surface area than the same mass of marble chips. ☐ ☐

e) A powdered solid reactant produces more product overall than an equal mass of reactant in large lumps does. ☐ ☐

Q4 Some reactions use **catalysts**. What is a catalyst?

....

....

Module C6 — Chemical Synthesis

Measuring Rates of Reaction

Q1 Complete the following sentence by circling the correct word from each pair.

> The **speed** / **volume** of a reaction can be measured by observing either how quickly the **products** / **reactants** are used up or how quickly the **products** / **reactants** are formed.

Q2 Charlie was comparing the rate of reaction of 5 g of magnesium ribbon with 20 ml of **five different concentrations** of hydrochloric acid. Each time he measured the volume of **gas** that was produced during the **first minute** of the reaction.

   a) In the space below draw the apparatus that Charlie could use to measure the **volume** of gas produced.

   b) Describe what Charlie could do if he wanted to follow the rate of reaction by calculating the change in **mass** over the course of the reaction.

   ....

   ....

   ....

Q3 Horatio was investigating the reaction between **lead nitrate** and different concentrations of **hydrochloric acid**. When lead nitrate and hydrochloric acid react they produce **lead chloride**, which is an **insoluble solid**.

   a) What name is given to this type of reaction?

   ....

   b) Describe how Horatio could measure the rate of reaction.

   ....

   ....

   ....

Module C6 — Chemical Synthesis

Alkanes

Q1 The ball-and-stick diagrams below show four different **hydrocarbons**.

a) i) Write the molecular formula and draw the structural formula for methane, ethane, propane and butane. Then draw lines to match each of these chemicals to its ball-and-stick representation. One has been done for you.

Name	Molecular formula	Structural formula	Ball-and-stick representation
methane	....		
ethane	C_2H_6	H-C-C-H (with H H above and H H below)	
propane	....		
butane	....		

ii) What name is given to this family of hydrocarbons?
....

b) When hydrocarbons are burned under certain conditions, only carbon dioxide and water are produced.

i) Write a balanced symbol equation (including state symbols) for the combustion of ethane (C_2H_6) under these conditions.
....

ii) Under what conditions must ethane be burned to form just these two products?
....

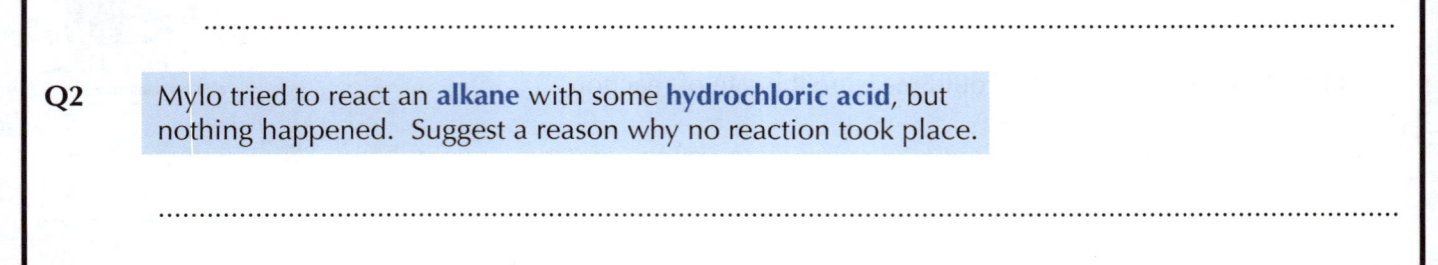

Q2 Mylo tried to react an **alkane** with some **hydrochloric acid**, but nothing happened. Suggest a reason why no reaction took place.
....
....

Module C7 — Further Chemistry

Alcohols

Q1 The **structural formulas** of alcohols can be used to identify them and determine their **properties**.

a) Circle any of the following molecular and structural formulas that represent alcohols.

C_4H_{10} H–C–O (=O, OH)   H–C–C–C–O–H (with H's) C_3H_7COOH H–C–C–C–H (with H's) $C_6H_{13}OH$

b) What is the functional group of alcohols?

....

Q2 Alcohols are used widely in the **chemical industry**.

a) i) Give the molecular formula of methanol.

....

ii) Give two uses of methanol.

1. ....

2. ....

b) i) Which alcohol is represented by the molecular formula C_2H_5OH?

....

ii) Give two uses of this alcohol.

1. ....

2. ....

c) All alcohols react in similar ways. Suggest a reason why.

....

Q3 Alcohols have some **physical properties** in common with other chemicals such as **water** and **alkanes**.

a) Tick the boxes to show whether the following are true or false.   **True   False**

i) Both water and ethanol are good solvents.   ☐ ☐

ii) Both water and ethanol are volatile at room temperature.   ☐ ☐

iii) Water, ethane and ethanol are all liquids at room temperature.   ☐ ☐

b) Describe what happens when sodium is added to ethanol, water and pentane (an alkane).

....

....

Module C7 — Further Chemistry

Carboxylic Acids

Q1 All **carboxylic acids** react in a similar way.

a) In the space below draw the structural formula of methanoic acid.
Put a ring around the functional group.

b) Suggest a reason why methanoic acid reacts in the same way as other carboxylic acids such as propanoic acid and butanoic acid.

....

Q2 Lizo is carrying out some experiments with **ethanoic acid**.

a) Give the molecular formula of ethanoic acid.

....

b) Lizo reacts ethanoic acid with the metal calcium.
The salt calcium ethanoate, $Ca(CH_3CO_2)_2$, is formed.

   i) What other product is formed in the reaction?

   ....

   ii) Write a balanced symbol equation for the reaction.

   ....

c) In another experiment the products of Lizo's reaction were sodium ethanoate, water and carbon dioxide. Suggest what Lizo has reacted the ethanoic acid with.

....

Q3 Beer or wine that has been left open to the air for several days often tastes like **vinegar**.

a) Explain why beer or wine that has been left open tastes like vinegar.

....

....

b) Give two other examples of unpleasant smells or tastes caused by carboxylic acids.

1. ....

2. ....

Module C7 — Further Chemistry

Esters

Q1 Hermione is a fragrance facilitator working for a **perfume manufacturer**. She frequently uses **esters**, since they are commonly used in perfume production.

  a) Give two properties of esters that make them suited for use in perfumes.

   1. ....

   2. ....

  b) Part of Hermione's job involves producing esters.

   i) Which of the following represents the correct reaction for the production of an ester? Circle the correct answer.

   alcohol + water → ester + carbon dioxide

   alcohol + alkane → ester + water

   metal oxide + carboxylic acid → ester + water

   alcohol + carboxylic acid → ester + water

   ii) What word describes a reaction that produces an ester?

   ....

  c) Other than perfumes, give two uses of esters in the chemical industry.

   1. ....

   2. ....

Q2 Complete the following passage using words from the box.

| esters | oils | unsaturated | double | energy | saturated | glycerol | single |

Animals that take in more .... than they need will store the excess as fat. Animal fats have mainly .... hydrocarbon chains — the bonds between the carbon atoms are .... bonds. Plants store any excess energy as .... with mostly .... hydrocarbon chains — meaning many bonds between the carbons are .... bonds. All fats and oils are .... of .... and fatty acids.

Top Tips: Esters really are great, but they don't only occur in industry. The smells and flavours of most fruits are caused by esters. Make sure you've got the basics under your hat, like the general word equation for the formation of an ester and all the different uses of esters.

Module C7 — Further Chemistry

Making an Ester

Q1 The production of pure **esters** involves a **multi-step** procedure.

a) i) Draw lines to match up the different stages in the production of ethyl ethanoate with the correct diagrams below. One has been done for you.

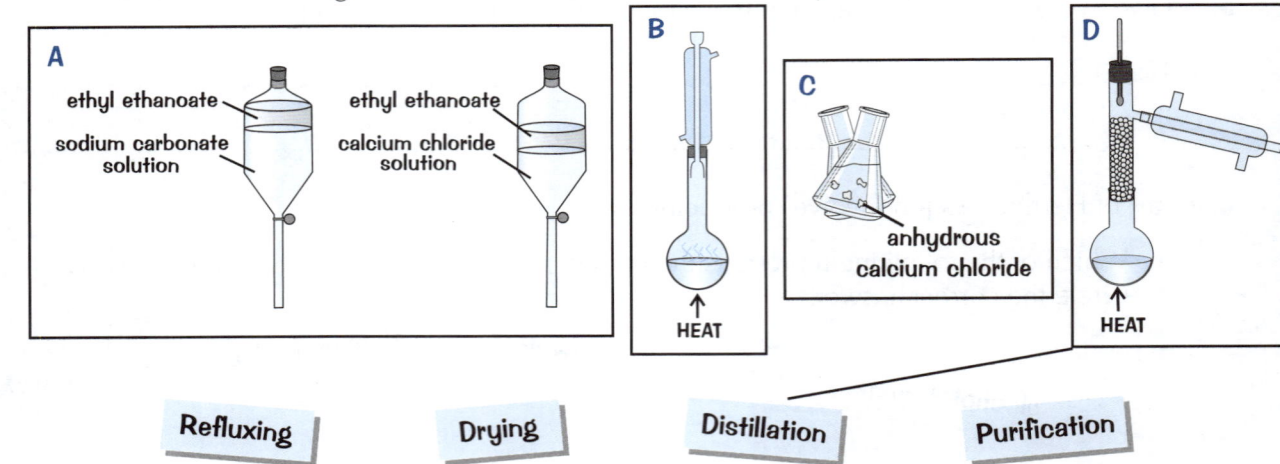

[Diagrams A, B, C, D shown: A — two tap funnels with ethyl ethanoate / sodium carbonate solution and ethyl ethanoate / calcium chloride solution; B — distillation flask with heat; C — conical flask with anhydrous calcium chloride; D — reflux apparatus with heat (linked to "Purification" — note: the line appears to join D to Purification as the example)]

Labels: Refluxing   Drying   Distillation   Purification

ii) Put the stages A, B, C and D in the correct order.

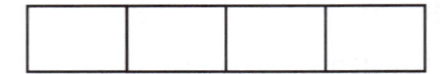

[ ] [ ] [ ] [ ]

b) What is the purpose of the distillation? Circle the correct answer.

- to purify the ester
- to separate the ester from the other chemicals in the flask
- to remove water from the ester
- to help the remaining alcohol and acid react

c) Complete the following passage by circling the correct word(s) in each pair.

> Purification is carried out in a **fractionating column / tap funnel**. The ester is shaken with sodium carbonate solution to remove the **acidic / alkaline** impurities. Then the sodium carbonate solution is tapped off. The ester is then shaken with concentrated calcium chloride to remove any **ethanol / acid**.

d) i) In diagram C, what does the anhydrous calcium chloride do?

....

ii) How are the solid lumps of anhydrous calcium chloride removed from the ester after this stage of the reaction?

....

e) i) During refluxing, why is sulfuric acid used?

....

ii) Why should the apparatus **not** be heated with a Bunsen?

....

Module C7 — Further Chemistry

Energy Transfer in Reactions

Q1 Use the words below to **complete** the blanks in the passage.

> endothermic   exothermic   energy   heat   an increase   a decrease

All chemical reactions involve changes in ....
In .... reactions, ... energy is given out to the surroundings. A thermometer will show .... in temperature.
In .... reactions, ... energy is taken in from the surroundings. A thermometer will show .... in temperature.

Q2 **Energy level diagrams** can be used to show whether a reaction is exothermic or endothermic.

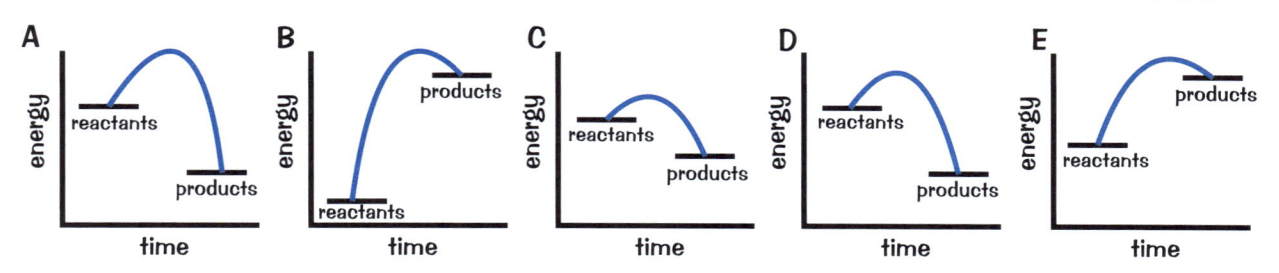

a) Which diagram(s) show:

   i) an exothermic reaction? ....

   ii) an endothermic reaction? ....

b) **i)** What is meant by the term activation energy?

   ....

   ii) Which diagram shows the reaction with the highest activation energy? ....

Q3 An **energy level diagram**, like the one on the right, can be used to calculate ΔH for a reaction.

a) What does the symbol ΔH represent?

....

b) What is the value of ΔH for the reaction shown?

....

c) What is the activation energy?

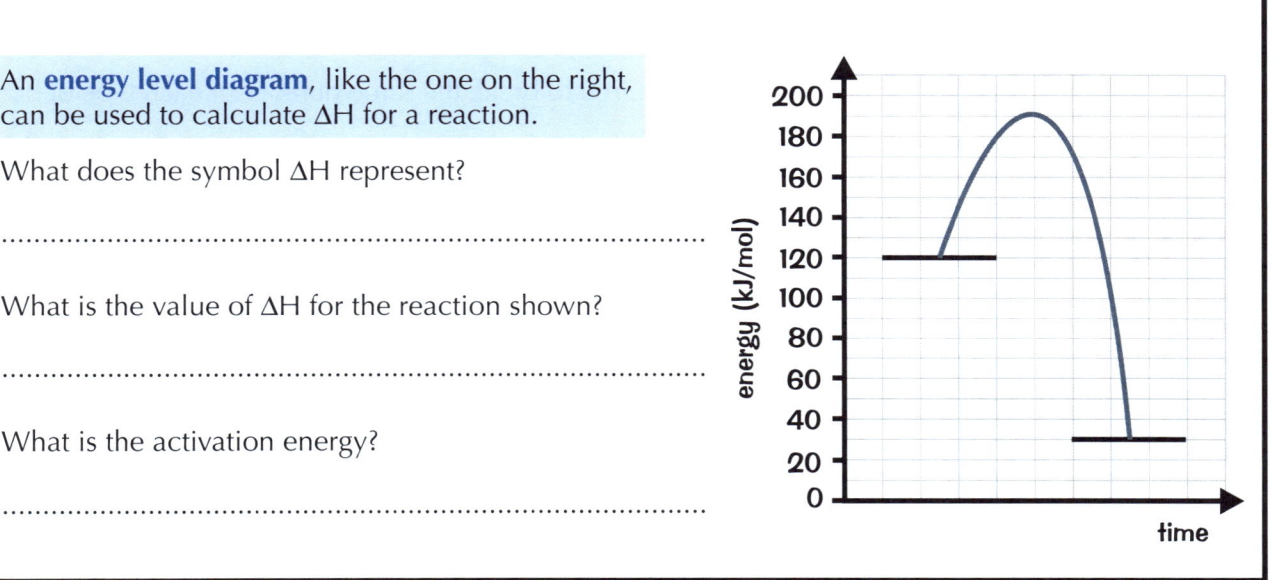

....

Module C7 — Further Chemistry

Catalysts and Bond Energies

Q1 Many reactions, especially those in industry, use **catalysts**.

a) What effect do catalysts have on chemical reactions?

....

b) The diagram opposite shows the same reaction carried out twice, once with and once without a catalyst. Use the diagram to explain how catalysts work.

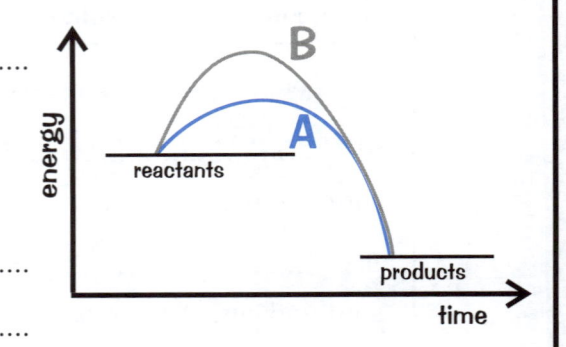

....

....

c) On the diagram, draw and label arrows to show the activation energy for the reaction without a catalyst and the activation energy for the reaction with a catalyst.

Q2 State whether bond **breaking** and bond **forming** are exothermic or endothermic processes. Give reasons for your answer.

Bond breaking ....

....

Bond forming ....

....

Q3 The equations below show a reaction between **methane** and **bromine**.

$$CH_4 + Br_2 \rightarrow CH_3Br + HBr$$

The figures below show the energy required to break the same number of each type of bond.

C–H = +435 kJ   Br–Br = +193 kJ   C–Br = +288 kJ   H–Br = +366 kJ

a) Calculate the energy change for the above reaction.

....

....

b) Explain whether this reaction is exothermic or endothermic.

....

Module C7 — Further Chemistry

Reversible Reactions

Q1 Use words from the list below to complete the following sentences about **reversible reactions**.

escape   reactants   catalysts   closed   products   react   balance

a) In a reversible reaction, the .... of the reaction can themselves .... to give the original ....

b) At equilibrium, the amounts of reactants and products reach a ....

c) To reach equilibrium the reaction must happen in a .... system, where products and reactants can't ....

Q2 Look at this diagram of a **reversible reaction**.

The reaction going from left to right is called the forward reaction.
The reaction going from right to left is called the reverse reaction.

a) For the forward reaction:
   i) give the reactant(s) ....
   ii) give the product(s) ....

b) Here are two labels:

   X product splits up
   Y reactants combine

   i) Which of these labels goes in position 1 — X or Y? ....
   ii) Which goes in position 2 — X or Y? ....

c) Write the equation for the reversible reaction. ....

d) Complete the sentence by circling the correct phrase.

In a dynamic equilibrium, the forward and backward reactions are happening:

at different rates / at zero rate / at the same rate.

Q3 The reactions below show the **ionisation** of two acids.

A: $HCl_{(aq)} \longrightarrow H^+_{(aq)} + Cl^-_{(aq)}$

B: $CH_3COOH_{(aq)} \rightleftharpoons H^+_{(aq)} + CH_3COO^-_{(aq)}$

Say which acid is strong and which is weak. Explain your answer.

....
....
....

Module C7 — Further Chemistry

Analytical Procedures

Q1 Analytical procedures can be **quantitative** or **qualitative**.

a) Describe the difference between quantitative and qualitative analysis.

....

....

b) Tick the boxes to show which type of analysis will tell you:

	Qualitative	Quantitative
i) the amount of oxygen present in air	☐	☐
ii) whether lead was present in a water sample	☐	☐
iii) the amount of iron in an iron ore	☐	☐
iv) the formula of a hydrocarbon	☐	☐
v) the number of different dyes in a food colouring	☐	☐

Q2 A scientist is investigating the level of **soil pollution** near a factory. The scientist digs a small hole, and collects a soil **sample** from a depth of about 10 cm. The scientist collects **two other samples** from nearby areas.

a) Suggest **two** reasons why the scientist collected three soil samples.

1. ....

2. ....

b) The scientist dissolves the samples in a solvent before analysing them.

i) Explain why the samples are dissolved in a solvent.

....

ii) Explain the difference between an aqueous and a non-aqueous solvent.

....

....

c) Suggest three reasons why the scientist follows standard procedures when analysing the soil samples.

1. ....

2. ....

3. ....

Top Tips: Qualitative and quantitative are two words that sound very similar but mean very different things — make sure you don't get them muddled up. The way I remember it is that **quant**itative is like **quant**ity, which is how much of something there is — I knew you'd see it my way.

Module C7 — Further Chemistry

Analysis — Chromatography

Q1 Look at the diagram of a **chromatography** experiment below.
Then tick the boxes to show whether the statements are **true** or **false**.

		True	False
a)	The sample dissolves in ethanol.	☐	☐
b)	Ethanol is an aqueous solvent.	☐	☐
c)	Ethanol is the stationary phase in this experiment.	☐	☐
d)	Paper chromatography is an example of quantitative analysis.	☐	☐

Q2 **Paper chromatography** and **thin-layer chromatography** both have **mobile** and **stationary phases**.

a) Complete the sentence by circling the correct word in each pair.

> Chromatography separates the components of a mixture as a
> **mobile / stationary** phase moves through a **mobile / stationary** phase.

b) Describe one difference between paper chromatography and thin-layer chromatography.

....

....

c) Complete the following passage using words from the box to describe what affects how far the different chemicals in a sample travel in paper chromatography.

further	more	mobile	stationary	distributed

Each component in a mixture is .... between the mobile and stationary phases. Components that spend .... time in the .... phase will be carried .... up the paper. Because the distribution of each component is different each one is carried a different distance by the solvent.

d) A dynamic equilibrium exists between the molecules in the stationary and mobile phases. Explain this dynamic equilibrium.

....

....

Module C7 — Further Chemistry

Analysis — Chromatography

Q3 A **food colouring** was analysed using **paper chromatography**. The chromatogram shown below was produced.

a) Spot A was a yellow dye, and spot B a cream-coloured dye. They were both difficult to see, so the chromatogram was treated to make the spots show up better. What could be used to do this? Circle the correct answer.

    A black dye   A colouring agent

        A locating agent   A solvent

b) Use the formula to work out the R_f value of each dye.

$$R_f = \frac{\text{distance travelled by solute}}{\text{distance travelled by solvent}}$$

   i) Dye A ....

   ii) Dye B ....

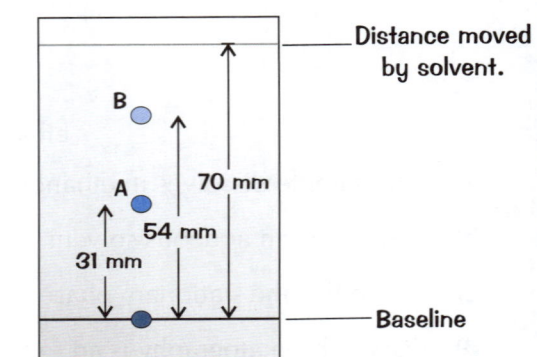

(Diagram shows: Distance moved by solvent = 70 mm, Spot A at 54 mm, Spot B at... 31 mm — baseline labelled.)

Q4 Substances can also be analysed using **gas chromatography**.

a) Outline how gas chromatography works.

....

....

....

b) Gas chromatography was used to analyse an unknown sample. The results are shown below.

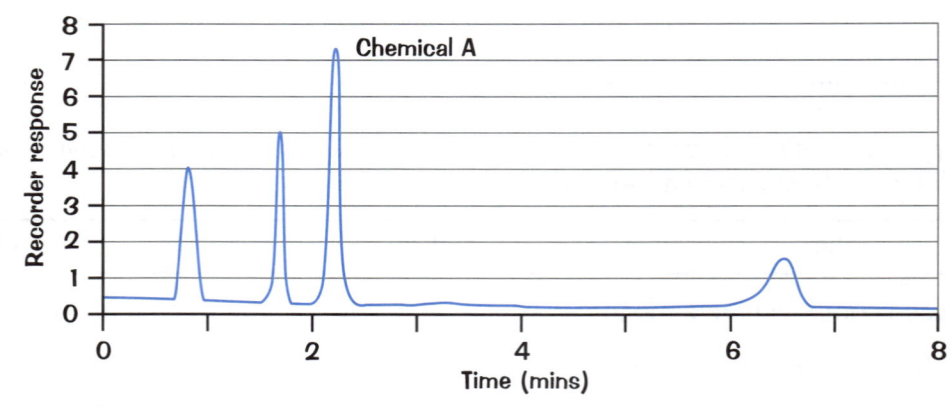

   i) How many different chemicals are in the mixture? ....

   ii) What is the approximate retention time of chemical A? ....

   iii) How can you use the retention time to identify the chemical? ....

....

   iv) How would you find out the amount of chemical A in the sample using the chromatogram?

....

Module C7 — Further Chemistry

Analysis — Solution Concentrations

Q1 Which of the following **isn't** a measure of **concentration**? Circle the correct answer(s).

l/dm³   g/dm³   grams per litre   mg/dm³

Q2 Use the formula below to solve the following problems.

concentration (g/dm³) = mass of solute (g) ÷ volume of solution (dm³)

a) Calculate the concentration of a solution made by dissolving:

i) 10 g of calcium carbonate in 1 dm³ of water.

....

ii) 1 g of sodium chloride in 20 cm³ of water.

....

b) Calculate the mass of solute in:

i) 2 dm³ of magnesium sulfate solution with a concentration of 10 g/dm³.

....

ii) 500 cm³ of copper carbonate solution with a concentration of 50 g/dm³.

....

Q3 A scientist wants to make 500 cm³ of a **standard solution** of sodium chloride with a concentration of 150 g/dm³.

a) How many grams of solute will the scientist need?

....

b) Put numbers in the boxes next to the following statements so they are in the correct order.

☐ Top the flask up with distilled water.
☐ Weigh out the mass of solute.
☐ Tip the solution into a volumetric flask.
☐ Stopper the flask and turn it upside down a few times.
☐ Rinse the beaker and stirring rod with distilled water and add the rinse water to the volumetric flask.
☐ Add a small amount of distilled water and stir until the solute has dissolved.

c) The volumetric flask has a line to indicate where it should be filled to. Describe **exactly** what the scientist will see when enough water has been added.

....

Module C7 — Further Chemistry

100

Analysis — Titration

Q1 Julia has a solution of **sodium hydroxide**, NaOH, with an **unknown concentration**. She carries out an **acid-base titration** using sulfuric acid, H_2SO_4, to determine the concentration.

a) What are each of the following items used for in a titration experiment?

   i) Burette ....

   ii) Indicator ....

b) The equation below shows the reaction that occurs during the titration. Balance the equation.

   .... NaOH(aq) + ... H_2SO_4(aq) → .... Na_2SO_4(aq) + ... H_2O(l)

c) The relative atomic mass of each of the elements present in the titration reaction are:

   sodium = 23, oxygen = 16, hydrogen = 1, sulfur = 32.

   Calculate the relative formula mass of:

   i) Sodium hydroxide, NaOH ....

   ii) Sulfuric acid, H_2SO_4 ....

The table below shows the results of Julia's titration experiments.

	Titration	1	2	3	4	Mean
Julia's solution	Volume of H_2SO_4 added (cm³)	31.0	27.3	27.5	27.4	

d) i) Julia decides one of her results is **anomalous**. Which titration produced her anomalous result? Give a reason for your answer.

   ....

   ii) Calculate the mean of Julia's **remaining** results and add the answer to the table.

   iii) How confident can Julia be that this result is accurate? Explain your answer.

   ....

   iv) The concentration of acid Julia used was 98 g/dm³. Calculate the mean **mass** of acid used.

   ....

   v) Use the following equation to calculate the **mass** of sodium hydroxide in Julia's solution.

   $$\frac{\text{mass of } H_2SO_4}{M_r \text{ of } H_2SO_4} = \frac{\text{mass of NaOH}}{2 \times M_r \text{ of NaOH}}$$

   ....

   vi) Julia used **25 cm³** of the sodium hydroxide solution in each titration. Calculate the concentration of the solution in g/dm³.

   ....

Module C7 — Further Chemistry

The Chemical Industry

Q1 The **chemical industry** is responsible for manufacturing products that we use every day.

   a) Complete the following passage about industrially produced chemicals using words from the box.

specialist	drugs	ammonia	small	large

   Fine chemicals include chemicals such as ....
   They're produced on a .... scale and require
   .... production. Chemicals such as
   .... require ....-scale
   production in the chemical industry — these chemicals are called
   bulk chemicals.

   b) Tick the boxes to show whether the products below are bulk chemicals or fine chemicals.

   Bulk Fine
   i) Sulfuric acid ☐ ☐
   ii) Fragrances ☐ ☐
   iii) Sodium hydroxide ☐ ☐

   Bulk Fine
   iv) Ammonia ☐ ☐
   v) Phosphoric acid ☐ ☐
   vi) Food additives ☐ ☐

Q2 Mike is the manager of a **chemical company** that produces **cleaning products**. The company is currently developing a new floor polish called 'In the Buff'.

   a) Sandra is a research scientist employed by Mike's company.
   Why is Sandra's role an important part of the 'In the Buff' team?

   ....

   b) The table below outlines four different processes that could be used to make the new floor polish.

Process	Raw materials cost (£m)	Running costs (£m)	Level of pollution created	Product (tonnes)
A	10	11	High	550
B	5	11	Moderate	600
C	21	7	Moderate	480
D	13	9	Very high	520

   i) What would the person in charge of operations use this table for?

   ....

   ....

   ii) The level of pollution created by process D is above the permitted limit set by the government. Explain why the government enforces regulations to control chemical processes.

   ....

Module C7 — Further Chemistry

Producing Chemicals

Q1 Producing chemicals involves several stages, as shown by the diagram.

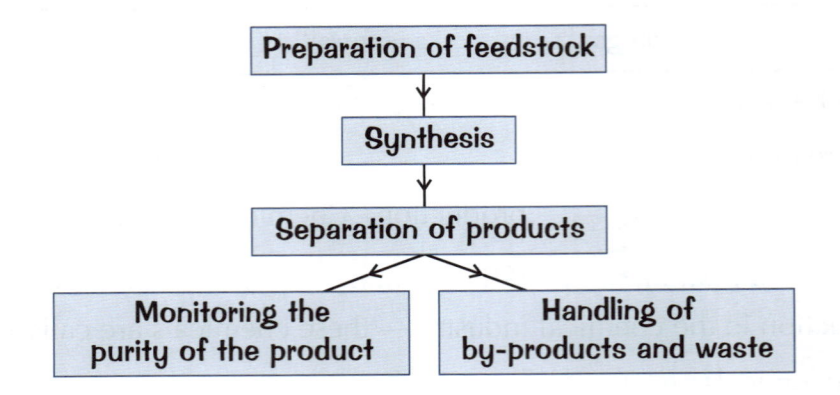

```
Preparation of feedstock
         ↓
      Synthesis
         ↓
Separation of products
    ↙           ↘
Monitoring the    Handling of
purity of the     by-products
product           and waste
```

a) In which stage are the reactants converted into products? ....

b) What does the term 'feedstock' mean?
....

c) Why is it usually necessary to separate the required product from the reaction mixture?
....

d) Explain why waste products must be disposed of carefully.
....

Q2 The flowchart below shows how **ammonia** is produced.

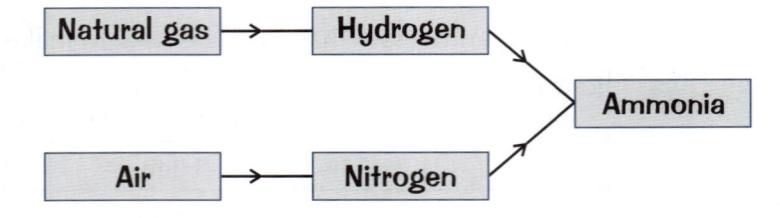

```
Natural gas → Hydrogen ↘
                        Ammonia
Air → Nitrogen ↗
```

a) i) Which two substances are the feedstocks? ....

ii) Which two substances are raw materials? ....

iii) Which substance is the product? ....

b) Explain why the conditions are carefully controlled during the synthesis of ammonia.
....

c) The word equation for the synthesis of ammonia is: Hydrogen + Nitrogen ⇌ Ammonia
Write a balanced symbol equation for the synthesis of ammonia (NH_3). Include state symbols.
....

Module C7 — Further Chemistry

Producing Chemicals

Q3 Millions of tons of **sulfuric acid** are produced every year for use in the chemical industry.

> 1. Sulfur is produced as a by-product of the purification of oil and gas.
> 2. The sulfur is burned in air to produce sulfur dioxide: $S(s) + O_2(g) \rightarrow SO_2(g)$.
> 3. Sulfur dioxide is converted to sulfur trioxide. The reaction is carried out at high temperature, using a catalyst to increase its rate: $2SO_2(g) + O_2(g) \rightleftharpoons 2SO_3(g)$.
> 4. Sulfur trioxide is dissolved in concentrated sulfuric acid: $SO_3(g) + H_2SO_4(l) \rightarrow H_2S_2O_7(l)$.
> 5. Water is added to produce concentrated sulfuric acid: $H_2S_2O_7(l) + H_2O(l) \rightarrow 2H_2SO_4(l)$.

a) What are the raw materials used in this process? ....

b) How good is the atom economy of this process? Explain your answer.

....

c) The formation of sulfur trioxide is exothermic. The waste energy produced is extracted and used to heat the sulfur dioxide and oxygen mixture. How does this benefit the **environment**?

....

d) Describe one other **benefit** of using this process.

....

e) Is this method sustainable? Explain your answer.

....

....

Q4 The following paragraph describes the **production of copper**.

> Copper is found in compounds within certain rocks buried deep underground. 190 tonnes of this rock, or copper ore, needs to be mined to produce 1 tonne of pure copper. Copper is extracted from the ore using a process called smelting. This involves heating the copper ore to a very high temperature, at which impure copper can be removed. The impure copper is then purified by electrolysis, which separates the copper from its impurities using electricity. The overall cost of producing pure copper is £650 per tonne. It can then be sold for around £4000 per tonne.

a) Suggest three reasons why copper production is not sustainable.

....

....

b) Suggest three benefits of copper production.

....

....

Module C7 — Further Chemistry

Making Ethanol

Q1 The **ethanol** in **alcoholic drinks** is usually made using **fermentation**.

   a) Use the words in the box to fill in the gaps in the passage below about fermentation. Each word may be used once, more than once, or not at all.

hot	alkaline	enzymes	temperature	sugars	acidic
pH	cold	concentration	30 °C		50 °C

   Fermentation is used to turn .... into ethanol. The reaction happens due to the action of .... found in yeast. The .... and .... need to be carefully controlled during the reaction. If the reaction is too .... it will be very slow, and if it is too .... the .... will be destroyed. The optimum is about ....

   The solution should be slightly ....

   b) The fermentation reaction **stops** when the **concentration** of ethanol reaches about 10-20%. Why is the concentration of ethanol that can be produced by fermentation limited?

   ....

Q2 Fermentation is not used for **large-scale production** of high quality **ethanol**.

   a) What is the raw material used in the industrial production of ethanol?

   ....

   b) Describe the steps taken to convert this raw material into the feedstock needed to produce ethanol.

   i) Step 1: ....

   ii) Step 2: ....

   c) Which of the following is the correct word equation for the reaction used to produce ethanol? Circle the correct answer.

   ethane + steam → ethanol

   ethanoic acid + steam → ethanol

   ethyl ethanoate + steam → ethanol

   ethene + steam → ethanol

   d) Suggest two uses of industrially produced ethanol.

   ....

Module C7 — Further Chemistry

Making Ethanol

Q3 An ethanol solution can be made **more concentrated** by the process of **distillation**, using the apparatus shown below.

   a) Give one example of a drink obtained by the distillation of an ethanol solution.

   ....

   b) Describe what happens at the following places on the diagram.

   A ....

   B ....

   c) Explain how fractional distillation works.

   ....

   ....

Q4 Ethanol can be produced by **fermentation** or by reacting **ethene with steam**.

   a) Tick the boxes to show whether each statement applies to the process of fermentation (F) or reacting ethene with steam (E), or both.

   F   E

   i) It uses renewable resources. ☐ ☐

   ii) The reactions in the process have a high atom economy. ☐ ☐

   iii) The process produces waste products. ☐ ☐

   iv) A lot of energy is needed to maintain the high temperature and pressure used. ☐ ☐

   b) Which of the two methods is more sustainable? Explain your answer.

   ....

   ....

Q5 Ethanol can be produced from **waste biomass**.

   a) **i)** Give the optimum **temperature** for this process. ....

   ii) Give the optimum **pH** for this process. ....

   b) Why are **GM bacteria** needed?

   ....

   c) Give one reason why producing ethanol from biomass is a **sustainable process**.

   ....

Module C7 — Further Chemistry

Nauru and the Phosphate Industry

Q1 Read the following article then answer the questions that follow.

We are all becoming used to hearing pleas from environmentalists about the need to reuse or recycle non-renewable resources. However, most people have little concept of the damage that the exploitation of natural resources can wreak, and find it easy to ignore the warnings. One group of people with first-hand experience of the devastation that can be caused by our consumption of such resources are the inhabitants of the tiny island of Nauru in the Pacific Ocean. The island contained deposits of phosphate rock — the raw material used in the production of phosphoric acid — but these deposits have disappeared after 90 years of intensive mining, leaving Nauru environmentally and economically crippled.

There is little recorded history of Nauru before the late 1800s. It is thought that the nation provided for itself through farming, fishing, and trade with nearby islands and passing ships. In 1900, phosphate rock was discovered on the island buried underground in ancient coral reefs. Mining of the rock began in 1906 and carried on until there was so little phosphate left that it became uneconomic to continue.

The mining on Nauru has left around 80% of the island uninhabitable, leaving the islanders clustered along the coastline. In addition, the lack of vegetation in the centre of the island means the air above it is consistently warm. This tends to prevent rain clouds forming over the island, leading to frequent droughts. The lack of available land and the unfavourable climate means that farming on Nauru is very difficult and islanders now import most of their food.

Despite the wealth generated by mining, the island has suffered financial hardship since the supplies of phosphate rock were exhausted. Nauru now has no natural resources suitable for trade and few alternative sources of income. For instance, tourism is not a viable option because of the damage to the landscape caused by the mining.

Phosphate rock is currently mined in America and Russia and some parts of Africa, where significant deposits remain. The demand for phosphate rock stems mainly from the production of phosphoric acid. There are many uses of phosphoric acid, including the production of fertilisers and insecticides, as a food additive (it gives the 'tang' to cola), for water softening and as a catalyst.

There are two methods used to produce phosphoric acid in industry. The first method involves adding sulfuric acid to phosphate rock to produce phosphoric acid and calcium sulfate. Calcium sulfate (or gypsum) can be used to make plaster of Paris instead of being wasted.

> calcium phosphate + sulfuric acid ⇌ phosphoric acid + calcium sulphate

The second method is to burn phosphorus in oxygen to produce phosphorus oxide, then to react the oxide with water.

> phosphorus + oxygen → phosphorus oxide
> phosphorus oxide + water → phosphoric acid

Both methods are able to produce large amounts of phosphoric acid, though the first method is cheaper to run, but provides a less pure product. The method chosen depends on the end use of the phosphoric acid produced — for example the second method is employed when the product is to be used as a food additive and must be pure.

The future of Nauru and its people is uncertain. The island has recently begun generating income by acting as a detention centre for asylum seekers wanting to settle in Australia. There have also been proposals to regenerate the island by importing soil to repair the damage caused by the mining. An alternative solution would be to rehome the Nauruans on a different island and leave Nauru to the forces of nature. Whatever becomes of Nauru we would all be wise to remember the consequences of overexploiting the Earth's resources.

Module C7 — Further Chemistry

Nauru and the Phosphate Industry

a) What is meant by the term 'non-renewable'?

　..

b) Suggest one benefit of phosphate rock mining to the people of Nauru.

　..

c) Describe one environmental and one economic disadvantage of the mining on Nauru.

　Environmental: ....

　..

　Economic: ....

　..

d) The equation below shows the reaction that occurs when phosphoric acid is produced from phosphate rock. Balance the equation.

$$\ldots Ca_3(PO_4)_2\text{(s)} + \ldots H_2SO_4\text{(aq)} \rightleftharpoons \ldots H_3PO_4\text{(aq)} + \ldots CaSO_4\text{(aq)}$$

e) Why is the manufacture of phosphoric acid said to be a 'bulk' process?

　..

　..

Incredible Bulk

f) Phosphoric acid is produced in an aqueous solution. Explain what this means.

　..

g) Phosphoric acid is a weaker acid than sulfuric acid. Which of these two acids will ionise more completely when mixed with water? Explain your answer.

　..

h) A fizzy drinks company wants to begin producing phosphoric acid at their factory to save money. Which of the methods described in the article should they use? Give a reason for your answer.

　..

　..

i) Phosphoric acid is used as a catalyst in the production of ethanol from ethene. How does a catalyst speed up a reaction such as this?

　..

Module C7 — Further Chemistry

Nauru and the Phosphate Industry

j) Evaluate the sustainability of the method used to produce phosphoric acid from phosphate rock by answering the following questions:

i) Will the raw materials run out?

....

....

ii) How good is the atom economy?

....

....

iii) What is done with the waste products formed?

....

....

iv) What are the energy costs?

....

....

v) Will it damage the environment?

....

....

vi) What are the health and safety risks?

....

vii) Are there any benefits or risks to society?

....

viii) Is it profitable?

....

ix) Is the process sustainable? Explain your answer.

....

....

....

Module C7 — Further Chemistry